Working (It) Out

A Spin Instructor's Guide to Creating Playlists for Efficiency in Your Work, Home, and Personal Life

J. Rico Blanco

D1536448

Cover Art by: Alex Blanco contact: info@alexthedesigner.com
Thank You Alex!

Dedication

To everyone I know and everyone I will know – to my parents for the gift of life, to my siblings for teaching me to share, to my partner for putting up with my minimalist efforts and sharing a love of music, to my children and grandson, to "my person" (you know who you are), to my running group the "Chicago Brunching Bandits," to my chosen family, to my group fitness managers, colleagues, and fitness class participants (especially spin participants), to my yoga teacher training teachers, to my mentors, to all the musicians, songs, and lyrics that move me, and to the universe for providing us with so much.

&

A special thank you to Larry Guthrie for helping me figure out the first component of the book's title while having martinis and chatting about the completed manuscript for which I didn't have a confirmed title. I owe you a homecooked meal.

About the Author

    J. Rico Blanco lives in Chicago, IL, with his partner, two dogs, two birds, and two mice. Sort of like a 2-2-2-2 breakfast combo. Blanco lives within proximity to his two grown children and grandson. Blanco works full-time in Healthcare Association Management and lovingly says that his side hustle in fitness is also his full-time job.

Table of Contents

INTRODUCTION

Life, let's ~~edit~~ the shit out of it, was going to be the original title of this book. However, as I developed the book's content and included some editing processes for my spin and group fitness playlists, I found it only fitting to motivate you via a portal that I am familiar with and that most of us can relate to. You see, there is no need to be an avid spin class participant or have ever taken a spin class because the foundations of spin can apply to daily goals and life. But I do recommend that you take a spin class at least once. Spin classes are fun and help us build endurance and strength. It's an overall great workout that is accompanied by a great playlist. Through my writing, we'll explore the foundation of a spin class and how music contributes to a great ride and can help motivate you in your work, home, relationships, and life.

Music

Music is accessible to all of us. For most, music can elicit a feeling, whether nostalgia for days past or happy or sad feelings. Music's power is undeniable, has supported us throughout our lives, and is the foundation of many multi-billion-dollar businesses and how we communicate. Music is so strong in its narrative that it supports various media, such as movies, documentaries, tv shows, sporting events, commercials, podcasts, major group fitness platforms, and for this book, our own life's playlist. Come on, admit it; you know what music motivates you, elicits a response, and gets you going. We all have that song, band, or musician that speaks to us. That gets our feet stomping and body moving. Throughout history, music has allowed us to narrate current situations. It is, in many ways, a historical document of our past. For example, when Martin Luther King was assassinated in 1948, Ms. Nina Simone created the lyrics for *Why? (The King of Love is Dead)*, it was a testament to the life that Dr. King lived and highlighted the many contributions Dr. King made in the movement towards de-segregation and equal rights. One did not need to live during that time to understand the tragedy it was to lose Dr. King, or to understand his purpose.

Music also supports our daily life; coincidentally, as I edit this portion of the book, I am sitting in a coffee shop two days after Halloween. The music playing is seasonal, denoting the gift-giving holiday season soon to arrive, making me think of gift lists and other associated activities. In a sense, it is a call to action. As music often does, it motivates us and prompts us to move. A spin class's music can range from Beethoven to today's top hits, music is timeless, and regardless of the era of its origin, it can still have that motivational ability it had in years past.

Why did I decide to write this book?

Suppose you're like millions of other people in the world and me. In that case, you have a "to-do list" so long that you don't even keep a list, it's all in your head, and sometimes, like me, it's on my calendar for both work and home life that keeps me in line. Sometimes, I feel like Andrea in the *Devil Wears Prada*, where Miranda Priestly, played by Meryl Streep, says to Andrea, "Did you fall down and smack your little head on the pavement?" If you can relate to this, then this book is for you! If you haven't seen the movie, stream it now, it's worth the watch. Also, the playlist is fantastic. My love of music, fitness, minimalism, and getting shit done has led me to write this book and share my ideas. In addition to the above, I have decided to write this book in response to friends, family, colleagues, and strangers asking me how I accomplished my goals. Having enjoyed writing but having not written a book, I didn't know where to begin, but I had a new plan set. Having no idea about where to start, I began to evaluate all the editing that I had done prior and noticed similarities in my editing process. As I researched and reviewed my past accomplishments, I realized that each achievement stemmed from a genuine desire for what I wanted. I have found some enjoyment in a facet of the required tasks to meet my goals. But knowing this wasn't enough or seemed to be the right avenue for delivering what I've learned. However, in my knowledge bank, I understood that one should write about what they know and, if possible, pair it up with something that brings joy.

For me, that joy comes in the form of writing, fitness, and music.

Throughout this book, I will use time-honored methods by quoting experts in the field of work efficiency, home organization (helping you whether you're into maximalism or minimalism), and relationships. But of course, adding my own spin on things. I'll place references to music throughout the book where I feel a song or lyrics may contribute to the idea I'm trying to share.

Additionally, as you read this book, you'll notice that I repeatedly use the same expressions or cues throughout this book, for example, such phrases or cues as "You can do it!", "Workdays have a beginning and an end ." Repeating these cues is intentional; as an instructor, we often cue form and process in the same way throughout a class, adding slight variations when needed, which you will also notice I do in this book. When thinking of cues, I like to think about the subtle way driving cues help us to navigate the city. When I think about driving a car and the universal signs that are associated with driving, I think of words and colors that indicate stopping, going, or caution. When we first learned how to drive, the symbols and words are new to us that accompany traffic rules. Eventually, they become so second place that we obey them without thinking. As a spin instructor, my body, movements, and language have to become this common representation of what to do, essentially using all three to express cues; as spin instructors, we learn how to command a room. You'll need to tackle self-doubt and find phrases that help you move in the right direction. Something that will come in handy as you learn to motivate yourself to change.

Is this another self-help book? I'd like to think so, and hopefully, in the form that I deliver it in, you'll find some value. Self-help can come in places where you least expect it; one of the first self-help books I have ever read is one that I'd beg my mom to read to me every evening before bedtime. My mom, tired from working and maintaining a household, would resist. Still, she would somehow find the energy to read my siblings and me *The Little Engine that Could* by Watty Piper.

As she read the book, although I knew the outcome, I'd still route for the engine to overcome her fears. Later, I'd be able to read the book on my own. Still, for now, my mom's voice and the story it told soothed me to sleep and somehow informed me that everything was going to be ok no matter what happened. I still own the original book that my mom read to me when I was a child; with its torn and tattered pages, I can still read clearly the little engine repeating to herself, "I think I can. I think I can. I think I can." until she could. This message resonated with me then and still does to this day and is the driving force in all that I do.

Chapter One - A Little About Me

"I wouldn't tell you about the things they put me through the pain I've been subjected to…Try walking in my shoes. Try walking in my shoes."

Walking in My Shoes – Depeche Mode

Over my lifetime, but most importantly, I have reinvented myself in so many ways over the last thirty years. During that time, my list of things to do just kept growing, and my time got monopolized with family, career, socializing, and the demands of everyday life.

During the last 15 years, I have obtained an undergraduate degree in psychology, RRCA coaching certification, American Council on Exercise Personal Trainer Certification, Madd Dog Spin Instructor Certification, Behavior Coach Certification, Les Mills instructor certifications, and Yoga Teacher Certification. Somewhere in between all those certifications, I also earned a master's degree in health administration, all while working a full and part-time job for which I still do to this day. Why two jobs, you might ask. To be honest, it's a bit of an installation of my mom's work ethic and the residual effects of making ends meet by being a single parent to my deceased brother's two children. But most of all, I believe it is because I am a firm believer in always having a side hustle. I will probably have a side hustle until the day I retire, and then still have a hosh-posh of activities that I enjoy.

In addition, to the above accomplishments, while working in healthcare association management, I opened and closed a yarn shop and found ways to challenge myself with things such as 365 days of writing poetry, learning to swim, and countless marathons. (which, if you don't know already, required tons of training time). Why do I list my accomplishments? Well, you see, I believe that most folks can relate and have a list as long or longer than mine, and one thing we have in common is that we get it done. Somehow, we find a way, whether it be efficient or by the edge of a stationary bike seat, we get it done. It has been a little of both for me, learning how to improve my process and becoming somewhat of an expert in time management and prioritizing those things that need to be done. Getting it done means that whatever was important to me or necessary, I would get it done. You might question what I mean by necessary; necessary to me, for example, is like maintaining employment with a job that we aren't completely happy with but keeping it to pay the bills or to get us closer to our goals. It takes grit. In Angela Duckworth's book *Grit*, she defines grit as the "passion and perseverance for long-term goals." I can relate closely to her definition, as I believe I have embodied it throughout my life with a you can do it attitude. Giving up isn't an option once I have made the decision.

When I think about grit, I think about a time when I was challenged with learning a new skill. Ever since I can remember, my mom crocheted, and like most folks who worked with yarn, sometimes you have to take a project apart because you skipped a stitch or had the sizing wrong. We in the knit crochet world call this "frogging"; it's when you rip out your work, so in your mind, it sounds like a frog, "rip it, rip it, rip it." When my mom did this, I'd sit next to her on the floor while she sat on the couch and wrap the unfastened yarn around the core of the yarn, creating a ball of yarn. On this particular occasion, I was at least five years old; I asked her if she could teach me how to make something. For which she quickly said "no ."Being one not to give up and wanting to know how to do this, I kept asking. So one day, I had worn my mother out with daily asks that she threw a ball of yarn at me and said, "Here have at is." I immediately responded by saying, "I need that thing" "What thing?" she replied. "That pencil thing," I answered back. She laughed and said that I couldn't have a crochet hook and that'd I'd have to figure it out. Well, that night, in the limited privacy of the room I shared with my siblings, I focused and, with my fingers, crocheted some rows into about a five-by-five inches semi-square. I say semi-square because it was definitely odd looking. The next day, I showed my mom, and she quickly yelled at me for going through her stuff. I immediately cried, exclaiming, "I didn't go through her stuff!" For some reason, she believed me and asked me to show her how I did it. She quickly called her crochet buddy over to see what I had done, and her buddy said, "Clara, just give him a damn crochet hook and show him how to use it." My mom showed me how to use it and cautioned me that my dad would be mad. My dad came home later that night, while I was already hours into my first project, looked at me, and said, "just don't do it in public."

There are many ways that I've learned to create efficiencies in my daily life; it helped that I am an avid reader and a seeker of knowledge in all things that could simplify my life. Through my reading, I have become well-versed in current trends and time-honored traditions, such as hygge lifestyle, minimalism, coaching, career growth, leadership, emotional intelligence, and other related subjects, which I hope to capture in this book. I'll reference and quote some of the great authors that I've come to know through my quest for knowledge. I'll reference things I have learned from others who have shared similar experiences and whom I admire for their courage and success. Looking back, I acknowledge that there was no handbook handed to me when I received guardianship of my brother's children. There certainly are no handbooks for all the challenges we endure in life, whether big or small; I hope that by sharing my story and anecdotes, I can help you edit the things that are within your control. I have visualized this book as a casual conversation between you and me, the reader. With that being said, you'll notice that throughout this book, there are opportunities for more concise language, but as we know that with all real-life conversations, there are additional words that lend to a more comfortable dialogue. For example, I had noticed this in emails I've sent, which became more evident when this wonderful boss brought it to my attention. Although she didn't discourage it, she mentioned that there is a time and place for it. To be exact, it was while we were discussing emails, she said that I had a "flowery way of delivering a message," which she often tried to adopt in her own messaging to try to get away from sounding unapproachable to sounding more like a friend in emails. Now don't get me wrong, she and I both agreed that this is only sometimes suitable for all matters of business, but, when possible, should be implemented.

This concept of a casual conversation was taught to me by a site visitor while I was on a site visit inspecting a medical education institution. In a previous role, I used to attend site visits of medical colleges and large institutions that provided oversight to graduate medical education. I was always impressed by the site visitors with whom I followed and facilitated these site visits; they were well-versed in their roles and efficiently handled such significant tasks. However, on one site visit, with a seasoned site visit professional, I remember something he said that resonated with me and that from that day forward started to use it in many situations and still use it to this date. You see, site visits are a time of increased stress; a college, program, or institution is being reviewed for outcomes, competency, and overall satisfaction of the population it serves. On this site visit, the grandfatherly site visitor said the kindest words to the board and leaders of the institution being inspected. To put them at ease, he stated, "we are here to have a nice conversation; we are not here to find what you are doing wrong; we are here to identify best practices, identify areas for improvement, and share best practices that we've learned from other institutions." Once he said these words, I quickly noticed a sigh of relief from the folks we were inspecting. This little moment created a casual yet professional atmosphere permeating the site visit. Having this knowledge, I'll lend an example of how I use a similar approach when interviewing prospective new employees. After the introductions, I informed them that they were here because their resumes spoke for themselves and that the in-person interview was an opportunity to have a friendly conversation and learn more about each other. I also use this approach when assisting others in chatting about their fitness and life goals.

At an early age, we are given the tools to edit successfully; for some, it was in elementary school that we were taught to stay within the lines or to learn the difference between their and there.

But for all intents and purposes, I'll take you to a time not so long ago, when as an adult, I had my first interview with the group fitness manager (GFM) who would set the stage for how I looked at all future editing endeavors. As part of my interview process, I had to create a 30-minute High-Intensity Interval Training (HIIT) class. After completing my assignment, I had to perform the instruction for the group fitness manager and two other fitness instructors; this not being my first time at the rodeo, the instructor commented on how I hit all the targeted muscle groups that one would want to have in a thirty-minute class. As the two instructors left the room, the GFM asked me to write down every word I would use to deliver the class and present it to her the next day. The process of writing my delivery for the class would be my final assignment before she hired me; the next day, I presented my beautifully handwritten instructions, and with a red pen, she put a strikethrough over 80% of the words that I had written.

I learned at that moment that there is so much that we add when we speak and to our lives that is unnecessary and can and should be edited out. After this thoughtful lesson, I realized that I had always been an editor in life but had never realized it until I started to reflect on past accomplishments and the edits that I had made at that moment in time. A great lesson learned, indeed.

Having been a coach, fitness, and spin instructor for many years, I have learned some valuable lessons, such as when delivering instruction, you don't speak over the music, you stick to the verbal and physical cues, you limit the chaos, and create a cohesive workout and in the case of this book, "a playlist." While creating a playlist, instructors rely on templates taught to them by brands such as Peloton, Cyclebar, or Soul Cycle or through certifications such as Madd Dogg certification; they are given the tools necessary to enhance or create their templates.

When designing a ride template, clarity of the workout is essential. You must determine how hard your riders will work, the desired goals and outcomes, what challenges will help a rider gain strength and endurance, whether there will be intervals, and that noticeable achievements are placed strategically throughout the ride. And most importantly, what music selection will you choose to support the ride? You may ask yourself how this translates to accomplishing work, life, and relationship goals. Well, that's where the translation of music and playlist templates comes in to organize and create the life you want to lead. Over my years of instructing fitness classes, I have found many parallels between spin and everyday life. Think of beginnings and ends – a calendar year has a beginning and an end, and so does your workday, as we'll discuss later. For you, this book is my practical, honest approach. This book is about information sharing, an opportunity to share tried and true processes that have worked for me. In this book, I'll reference the techniques that have worked for me and share the information I've read or heard from experts in the field. We'll also discuss gratitude in the form of our approach, James Clear quotes in Atomic Habits "imagine changing just one word, you don't have to, you get to," for example "I have to go to work, to I get to go to work." Consistency drives change, and in your life, reminders are necessary. You can do it!

This is a fitness book for the mind. I hope that by sharing my knowledge, it will help you to generate your own ideas and create your own path, and essentially your own playlists. You can do this!

Chapter Two - You Can Do This!

"Pump up the jam, pump it up
While your feet are stompin'
And the jam is pumpin"
Pump Up the Jam – Technotronic

Yes, I know that we all have self-doubt, that new things are scary, and that previous failures resurface when we start something new. We have all failed and have survived setbacks and heartbreaks. So let's "Pump Up the Jam." Before I begin to motivate in my usual "you've got this" instructor voice and demeanor, I want to tell you about my first spin class experience. As with most experiences or challenges, it can stem from having the desire to learn something new, gravitate towards a group of people, or in my case; it was being invited to join a friend at a spin class which also intrinsically included the first two reasons that I listed above. When accepting the early morning spin class invite, I recognized that I was already used to waking up early on the weekend for a run with my running group and, at times, even earlier for longer runs spanning 15 or more miles. But waking up earlier on a weekday before work to workout was going to be a challenge. I had tried this when I was younger without much success, and I wasn't sure I was ready to try this again. With a bit of humor and in my best Sofia from the *Golden Girls* imitation, I'd start by saying, "Picture it 5:45 AM spin class, Sicily, umm, I mean Chicago".

So, on an early Tuesday morning, with no idea what to expect, I met my friend Lauren at 5:45 AM at Soul Cycle, where we were cheerfully greeted by very awake enthusiastic, friendly young front desk representatives, who checked us in and handed me a pair of rented cycling shoes. As I started to dress, my senses came alive, and the familiar scent of a mix of sanitizer and sweat permeated my nose. More than

11

likely, the sweat was from the participants in the earlier class who were exiting the cycling studio. As Lauren and I move through the brightly lit unisex locker area, I notice that every body type is imaginable, organically getting ready for the next class. At the same time, those before sharing the energy of the ride, the soon-to-be riders, share in the same energy, chatting away and pumped up on adrenaline. As Lauren leads me to the barely lit cycling studio, I notice words of encouragement such as "you are strong," "community," "rise", painted on the walls (these may not be the actual words, as it has been awhile since I've been there, and can't recall) but you get the gist; as I walk closer to the semi-darkened room a neon sign tells me that I'm going in the right direction. With every step, my anxiety builds, and my heartbeat joins in tandem. Upon entering, I noticed that the bikes are weirdly placed close to one another, and I noticed some very fit people already seated in the front row of the class; well, heck, throughout the class, there were fit people. You noticed that I said every body type is represented; just like runners, spin cyclists come in many forms, and just like runners, when we run, we are ready to bring it 100%.

I could tell that these folks were ready to bring it too. Each bike is numbered, and Lauren assists me in finding and setting up my bike, adjusting the handlebar and seat height to levels that fit my height and overall body, and asking if this or that felt too high or too far apart. Finding the right balance, and as I begin to mount the bike, my heart begins to race more; I shakily clip into the bike pedals, fearing that if I move to either side, I will ultimately fall off and onto the girl on either side of me, or worst, not be able to get out of the pedals. Because falling off wasn't an option because clipping out of the bike pedals wasn't previously an easy task when I rode my road bike. Expecting Lauren to sit next to me, I am surprised when she immediately rushes to the front row and clips herself into a bike front and center!!!! As we wait for the class to start, I am trying not to stare and attempt to fend off any obvious facial expressions that would give my fright away, I quickly glance around and can feel the confidence of each rider, eventually catching a glimpse of another novice spin participant and we share a look of concern and terror for what we are about to experience. The instructor walked in, and there was a collective sigh of awe; it was as if the whole room exhaled, which I didn't understand, but it would become apparent later. The instructor dims the lights, and the dimly lit colored lighting, barely noticeable before, is enhanced by the renewed darkness that overshadows the room. As the instructor takes his place on the podium and mounts his bike, the contours of his arms and chiseled face are highlighted by the overhead light above his head. Now I understand the exhale and the sigh. The playlist begins, and we are instructed to take all the resistance off our bike by turning the center knob to the left, slowly adding resistance as we warm up and increase speed. As the first track ends, we are instructed to slowly increase resistance as we move seamlessly into the next track and our first climb. We are then cued to rise up out of the saddle and continue to stay with the beat of the music, side to side, left to right, one two, one two. But here's the real deal, I am already tired and out of breath, and my heartbeat is beating like I'm racing a relay. As I struggle, Lauren looks back and shines the biggest smile, and in return, I fake an enthusiastic smile, and when she turns back to face the front, the same out-of-breath look returns to my face. Throughout the ride, I am questioning my ability to finish the remainder of the 50-minute class. However, I guess the instructor didn't think I was suffering enough and decided to approach my bike and add a full turn for more resistance. Please note that this doesn't usually occur in spin classes. Still, each studio has its own format, and instructors are coached to coach riders in a manner that is conducive to the rider and overall class experience. As the increased resistance slows me down, I find that I am once again in tandem with the beat of the music.

Then something magical happens; my ears, lungs, and heart open. I begin to fully hear the music, slowing or increasing my breath and effort to the music. I was innately preparing to adjust my resistance as the music changed within each track and increasing or slowing my speed to meet the beats per minute, which I would later find out translates to reps per minute.

As the ride continued, the music began to lift and motivate me to the end of class. I had done it; I finished my very first spin class. I believe that it helped that I was no stranger to the art of music, music has always played a key role in my life, and I was often woken up as a kid to my mom jamming out to her vinyl records. Which usually meant that she was cleaning, and we, her kids would soon be asked to join her in tidying up. If it wasn't to clean, it was definitely an opportunity to join her in dancing to the music, dancing to music was big in my family's home and still is something that we do to this day.

In life, there will be challenges, and I want you to know that, just like me, you can get through those challenges. In the above example, I demonstrate that something that started scary and challenging ultimately became something I mastered and sought to share with other riders and the reader. What at first seemed to be a challenge ended up being one of the most valuable experiences I've had. This story is it for now regarding my first experience with spin. However, I'll share a bit more about how I became a spin instructor later in the accountability chapter.

Throughout this book, I hope to embody many of the aspects of one of the first self-help books I've read as an adult, in Elaine St. James' book *Simplify Your Life: 100 Ways to Slow Down and Enjoy the Things That Really Matter*, she provides us with ideas on how to simplify our lives through short chapters with simple exercises, habits, and routines that will help us achieve success. In writing this book, I want you to see this book as vignettes of short quick chapters that pack a subtle, powerful punch to get you started right away.

I also want to take a moment to recognize Brene Brown and her attention to playlists. Brene Brown has a wonderful Podcast aptly titled *Dare to Lead*; in her podcast, at the very end of an interview with a guest, she asks the guest what "five songs they could not live without?" Each person provides a unique list of five songs that motivates and inspires them, their own personal playlist—further supporting the concepts that I have provided in this book regarding how music plays an essential part in motiving us and helping us through the components that I have presented in this book.

Some things to ask yourself while reading this book are:
- — What kind of employee am I?
- — What kind of home do I want to have?
- — What kind of person do I want to be with my family and friends?
- — Who do I want to be?
- — What is my own personal playlist?

But most importantly, I want you to rethink your identity, to take the best of who you are and, add to your already incredible unique self.

Chapter Three - Showing UP!

"It's just another manic Monday, I wish it was Sunday, Cause that's my fun day, It's just another manic Monday."
Manic Monday – The Bangles

When showing up, I want you to think of saying this in a Scooby Doo voice, "Showing UP!" Emphasis on "UP." So that it'll sound like "Showing RUP!"

Like your workday, a spin class has a beginning and an end. With the COVID-19 pandemic and more people working from home, the line of when your workday ends can be slightly blurred, for which we'll talk about boundaries later. But first, we must talk about showing up. You've already told yourself that you can do this, and now it's time to do *That Thing You Do.* "You doing that thing you do," lyrics by The Wonders.

For most of us, a fantastic, too-short weekend is had. Then Monday rolls around, and you find it hard to get out of bed; you're thinking about emails and looming deadlines that await you. Even if you love your job, there's heartache and heartache in the form of meetings, projects, coworkers, deadlines, and challenges. For later, we'll use this anxious energy to channel conquering vibes. I want you to keep in mind that Monday is a state of mine.

If you listen to the whole song *Manic Monday* by The Bangles, you'll realize that many of us share the same fear of being late or wanting to lay in bed and dream a little more. Sometimes showing up is the biggest battle you'll have to overcome for that day. Often, when I'm teaching/instructing a super early morning class, my initial response is one of trepidation, and depending on whether I got a good night's sleep, it can be just moments before I am fully awake and ready to teach. But through this, I have found that morning rituals are so important, even if it means haphazardly moving through a darkened room to get ready. For me, it's that moment I enter the bathroom, to the dimmed light I set the night before. The dimly lit room allows me to slowly wake, brush my teeth, and wash my face. There are no showers on the mornings that I teach because I'm going to be on a podium and away from the class participants, and the sweat will flow (and they can't smell me, at least I think they can't). Besides, and often, the class I taught the night before warranted a shower before going to bed.

Morning routines are crucial in creating habits. As James Clear has eloquently put it, "preparation is key; one habit forms another." Prior to becoming a fitness instructor, I struggled with the showing up part, I'd make a list of goals that I would want to accomplish, lose weight, gain muscle, eat better, etcetera, and for each one, I'd set a deadline, an insanely inaccurate deadline, to go along with my non-specific goal. Meaning that it was ok to say I'd lose weight but didn't attach the "how"; I was going to lose weight. Saying I'll show up at 6:00 AM for a spin class wasn't enough. I had to think about how I would get there, would I ride with a friend, catch public transportation, carb load the night before, and once there, what was expected of me? Of those mentioned above, the "how" and "what was expected of me" is already decided for you. The instructor outlines the class, and you ride along. Even with that part being determined for you, we still get caught up in what happens before you arrive. Where will we find the motivation to show up? Even before you arrive at the gym or spin/cycle studio, the efforts you make are crucial to setting you up for success. These are the most important things you'll do before that you want to make as simple as possible.

In addition to my bathroom routine mentioned above, I layout or pile my workout clothes on my desk, yep, piled; no one said that it had to be neatly organized, as long as my socks, shorts, t-shirt, and bandanna are all together I still accomplish getting ready for class. In addition, I set my coffee maker the night before. As I walk to the bathroom, I can smell the coffee that permeates the air and arouses my senses, serving the same purpose as my alarm clock, alerting me that it's time to get moving. While sipping my coffee, I am subsequently warming my throat, getting my voice ready for the microphone. All senses are awake, and I am mentally, physically, and emotionally prepared to instruct. I realized that to be a good instructor, not only did I have to learn formats and create playlists, I had to become it and do all things necessary to have me perform at my highest quality to be a good instructor. I don't play house; I become the house! Become that employee; become that person who is organized.

Do it once, and you have become it.

In *Atomic Habits*, James Clear gives an example that'll I would like to share with you.

"Imagine two people resisting a cigarette, when offered to smoke the first person says no thanks, I'm trying to quit, it sounds like a reasonable response but this person still believes that they're a smoker who is trying to be something else, they're hoping their behavior will change while carrying around the same beliefs, the second person declines by saying no thanks I'm not a smoker, it's a small difference but this statement signals a shift in identity. Smoking was part of their former life, not their current one, they no longer identify as someone who smokes."

It really is about habit formation and setting yourself up for success. Think about *Spiderman*, before he got bit by the spider, he was just your regular teenage high schooler with a crush. Once bitten, he became Spiderman. "Spiderman, Spiderman, does whatever a spider can. See what I did there? I just sang the Spiderman theme song to demonstrate how music can support a theme or an idea. The theme song also made him accountable for being Spiderman. I'll touch more on the idea of becoming in the Accountability chapter.

Chapter Four - The 3 D's Disrupt, Dismantle & Detach

"We're not gonna take it, No, we ain't gonna take it, We're not gonna take it anymore" *We're Not Gonna Take It* - Twisted Sister

As in the lyrics above, one must decide that they are "not gonna take it" and that they are ready to disrupt, dismantle, and detach from old habits and inefficient ways of doing things. The above three words are more powerful than you think; however, each looks pretty similar in its action. Each can be separated and applied to daily habits, relationships, and existing processes. I am providing Webster's dictionary definitions for each to understand each better.

— *Disrupt* – to break apart: to throw into disorder: to interrupt the normal course or unity of: to cause upheaval in (an industry, market, etc.).

— *Dismantle* – to disconnect the pieces of, also: to destroy the integrity or functioning of.

— *Detach* – to separate especially from a larger mass and usually without violence or damage.

when we dismantle, we must detach from something we already set in motion, including a person, place, or thing we've identified.

As mentioned above, the disruption would be required to flip the switch; it is the key to starting anew. An example that supports disruption is something I can relate to in my having dabbled in tarot card reading; disruption can be compared to the death card. The death of something old and the start of something new, for all intended purposes, a disruption. A clearly identifiable time that you can refer to and see progress made. Another example is movie ending credits, which dictate that something has ended and something new is on the horizon. When a movie ends, we can notice a disruptive event; the movie disrupted our previous knowledge. It is the start of new knowledge and power; like the heroine, we move forward into the sequel or the next chapter of life.

Now, for a bit more about Disrupt, Dismantle, and Detach.

Disrupt

Whitney Johnson's podcast *Disrupt Yourself* starts with the lyrics, "How will you disrupt yourself." With a 4.9-star rating, it is apparent that her podcast is thriving and that disruption is key in making changes happen. Johnson interviews guests and discusses strategies and advice on how to disrupt who you are. Many episodes come to mind, but one, in particular, is the interview with Susan McPherson: *Rising Above Disruptive Forces*, where author Ms. McPherson shares details of losing her mom to a horrible tragedy when she was 20 years old, stating "this completely disrupted my life, and obviously everyone else close to her," which started her "on a road to resolve and resiliency and making it work." When I heard this, it immediately resonated with my experience of losing my brother when he was 25 and I 23; losing him in such a tragic way disrupted and changed my life. From that day forward, my life was disrupted, and I resolved to live life to the fullest and ultimately changing the trajectory of the course that I was on, and then disruption again some years later when I took guardianship of his children. Needless to say, I continue to find gratitude for every year I have, and I currently outlive my brother and dad, who died when he was 48.

Recently, while hanging with a friend, he mentioned that another friend had heard that I was taking piano lessons. For which the friend asked my friend, I wonder why Rico keeps himself busy. "What is he running away from." You may have noticed that I didn't put a question mark after this quote because I believe it to be more of a statement said with what the friend felt was textbook psychology. Well, in any case, I

20

told my friend that when given the opportunity, he should tell our friend that I said I'm not running away from anything, that I am actually running towards something, that something is living life to the fullest. I can't outrun death, but I should the heck am going to enjoy every moment of this life that I have.

Dismantle

"I've been burning the candle at both ends (I'm going crazy)" "Trace the lines and find out where they lead" – *Dismantle Me* Ghost Key

Regarding the above, we should think about this a bit more, you and me, the reader.

When I was a child, I went around the neighborhood garbage picking, and believe me, and this was no term that my family and friends embraced. Garbage picking is when you pick through other people's trash and find hidden treasures; at least, I thought I was treasure hunting. But if I knew what I know now, I could've coined the phrase "upcycling." There are many different reasons one may garbage pick; as mentioned above, I did it for the treasures, but some people rely on it for survival, where someone finds and creates meals out of what they've been able to source by dumpster diving.

You can actually furnish your first home by dumpster diving (garbage picking). Still, as mentioned above, it was about finding treasures, finding old kitchen appliances, radios, and televisions, and then taking them back home to dismantle. In this case, I was dismantling something that was broken and discarded by its previous owner. Often, I have found that it was a quick fix of a loose wire and, in other cases, a more in-depth fix of needing salvaged parts from other similar items. Without really knowing it at the time, this process of investigating and dismantling would become my mantra when fixing work and life challenges. In a similar fashion, I would identify the issue, research what has worked for others, and then implement it by inserting new ideas into an existing process.

In this book, I will ask you to do the same with your workday, home, and life.

Detach

"One Don't Pick up the phone
You know he's callin because he's drunk and alone
Two: Don't let him in
You have to kick him out again
Three don't be his friend
You know you're gonna wake up in his bed in the mornin
And if you're under him, you ain't getting over him."
New Rules - Dua Lipa

As in Dua Lipa's lyrics above, we all have something we want to break up with, whether it's a habit, a partner, a job, a goal, or for the purpose of this chapter, let's break up with technology.

Specifically, the phone. While sitting at the coffee shop, I've noted that most patrons either have a laptop out or are intently staring at their phone screens and, in some cases, looking away from their laptops to consult their phones.

I used the word consult because the phone has evolved from taking calls and receiving text messages to being more than that by providing the universe at our fingertips—a technological consultant. Our phones have become a tool to communicate and share information in the most efficient on-demand way possible; it has become an invaluable component of our world. In the same way that it helps, it can also become a major deterrent in productivity or expose us to unwanted cyber situations. But for the purpose of this chapter, I want you to think about this, have you ever picked up a phone and had it opened and in mere seconds have forgotten why you went to it in the first place? The phone is today's modern analogy of walking into a room and forgetting why you entered the space in the first place.

In my case, I had to learn to master the technology provided at our fingertips and tackle the phone and how it is used, especially when it has indirectly become part of our workday.

Breaking up is hard to do, so hold on to your phone and start by saying it's not you; it's me. Wait, nix that, it actually is your phone, or could it be like in most relationships? We attempt to mold our partner into our ideal partner. There's an old saying that goes something like this, I love you, don't ever change, then somewhere during the relationship, you ask for change, for compatibility, and in some cases, the change is too significant that you must break up. Now think of your phone as that bright shiny brand-new relationship, where you wait up all night till the latest version is available the following day, and you rush to the store to purchase it, or like many, you've fallen victim to cellular providers offering you an upgrade and pre-ordered the latest version. We approach phones like relationships, expecting them to fulfill our needs and hoping that this newest version will be the one. But then we are alarmed when a shinier new version arrives. Each version promises us greater functionality, so we set high expectations when the factory settings of applications (apps) have been slightly enhanced. The basic apps form the anatomy of the phone, such as a new camera, email, text messaging, and high-speed internet; you get the gist. In addition to these apps, somewhere along the way, you get an invite for an app; in my case, it was Words with Friends; now, just to let you know, I haven't given up the Words with Friends app because the person on the other end means the world to me. It's a nice way for us to stay connected and disrupt our day by challenging our word knowledge. Heck, I'd venture to say that it has even assisted me in writing this book. It so happens that there are so many apps out there and so many connections that the phone helps to maintain. When used appropriately, it can be healthy; however, if not managed properly can be detrimental. When it becomes detrimental, it hinders you from doing what you've set your mind to, whether it be work, house chores, getting to sleep early, etc.

You noticed that I said to avoid and not stop; as mentioned earlier, finding moderation is key, and some apps or processes are necessary elements of daily life. With that being said, you must remember that the phone can be a valuable resource. Still, it can also be an enabler of habits that you are trying to avoid.

Through baby steps, I enabled myself to do more and not let my phone wreak more havoc than it already had. First, I organized my phone apps into pods. Below are ten that might apply to you, but remember, those that you need quick access to, should be placed on your home screen.

— Finances – Bank, Credit Cards, Mortgage, Auto Loan, Student Loan, and personal lines of credit.

— Travel – Airlines, Travel apps, commuter, and parking apps

— Phone Installed Apps – These are usually the ones that are presented with your IOS or Droid phone, such as the app store, health apps, photos, reminders, music, and notes.

— Stores & Services – Amazon, Fuel Rewards, Cell phone provider, frequently visited stores (i.e., Target, Michaels, Blick), services such as Dolly, Yelp, and other food delivery services.

— Utilities – Calculator, measuring tape, voice memos.

— Social Media – Facebook, Instagram, etcetera.

— Entertainment – Music Apps, Streaming Apps, Gaming, Book (audio or readable), Words with Friends, etc.

— Fitness & Wellness Apps – NikeRun, Garmin, Yoga, Gym Membership Apps

— Educational – School Affiliated Apps,

— Work Apps – this one I left for last because this can be a tough one in our connected world.

When reviewing your apps, I want you to think about which ones lend to good habits and which ones lead to bad habits; it's about finding balance. Do what helps you find balance. You can break it down into good and bad apps. We'll talk more about balance later in this book's "Components of a Ride" portion. Once you have broken down the apps you are keeping, try to monitor your use, and then subsequently delete those that you find you don't use often or that no longer contribute to that point in time. For example, when I paid off my auto loan, I immediately deleted that app, and when I was done with school, those apps went away.

In addition to the above, I implemented one extreme that has benefited me tremendously. I have silenced my text message notifications; it is completely turned off, meaning that I get no alerts, no screen notifications, and no dings, which means no interruptions and that I only view my text messages when I want to. Returning text in one big swoop. Another extreme has also been turning off notifications for my *Gmail* and *AOL* email accounts. Convenient and efficient. Lessor extremes would be turning off notifications for "Words with Friends," department store notifications, and other alerts that may pop up—additionally, reevaluating how many email accounts you may have. When email providers were limited, most of us had one email address. Still, as situations change, you may have added a new email account like most. I keep two for various reasons, but with a little bit of effort and moving information around, I could narrow it down to one. But I keep two because the old data I might need to access is definitely on the AOL email account, and I'm not ready to break-up with either email account.

Detaching from Home Stuff

In the words of Etta James, "Something's gotta hold on me," and it definitely does; for most of us, detaching from home stuff can be a rather difficult task; if it weren't such a difficult task, we'd all be living a minimalist lifestyle or having organized maximalists' homes. For some, Marie Kondo's method of "does this spark joy?" works; for others, it takes a different approach. There are many different approaches out there; for example, in *Minimalist Home*, author Joshua Becker says that "there is something refreshing and life-giving about a clean and uncluttered kitchen." I agree with this, but I also believe this concept applies throughout every room in your house. Especially those that are often inhabited, like the kitchen.

Becker also refers to an article in the New York Times titled *A No-Frills Kitchen Still Cooks*, where writer Mark Bittman breaks down the necessary kitchen appliances we need and lists those we often buy but don't need—finding kitchen utensils and tools that serve multiple purposes. For a more in-depth review of the article, please visit the references listed at the back of this book. In Etta James' lyric above, something has a hold on us.

We give value to material possessions which only increases their hold on us. Sometimes, we have to see each item for what it is, ask whether it's practical or has been used recently, and then quickly dispose of it. In the Dismantle portion immediately preceding this Detach portion, I gave an example that I was able to take discarded small appliances and make them new. Eventually, this hobby led to many black-and-white televisions, radios, VCRs, and other small devices. Eventually, I had to detach from these trophies of my resourcefulness and genius (ok, probably not a genius, but some smarts nonetheless), possessions that I valued because I had put so much time and energy into them.

They all had brought me joy, but I knew I had to depart with them. I eventually sold some and gave away items, bringing joy to others while cleaning up the limited space I had at home.

Detaching from Family and Friends

I left detaching from family and friends for last because this will be the most difficult one. I agree with Sarah Knight; in the outline of her book *The Life-Changing Magic of Not Giving a F*ck*, she saves her chapter on family and friends till the last portion of the book. With work, you can always make changes, and I mean always; there is always going to be an alternate way or approach, and it is something we can recover if lost. It won't be easy, but it'll pass, and new jobs and skills will present themselves. For our home, it's a material possession. We may even love where we live, but things happen, and living situations change, and somehow, we recover what is lost and, in some cases, are better for it. But relationships can be tricky and sometimes take a bit more courage. There are many books on relationship salvation, breaking up, and preservation of relationships that could use some strengthening. I am not an expert; however, my experience has helped me navigate the ins and outs of my relationships. From having a close family member with dissociative identity disorder, challenges in long and short-term relationships, and the toxicity of divorce parents. Let alone my own inherent issues that I bring to my relationships. Now for what has worked for me. With family and friends, we can experience moments of clouded judgment where we are unable to make clear decisions, decisions that are difficult because the decisions are tied to love, family bonds, years of friendship, and in some cases, just the history shared with a particular person. Being one of five children in a two-parent household before my parent's divorce, we learned to accept difficulty from others, share space, and allow for some disruption and angst.

However, as adults, we have more control over the creation of the environment where we live and the spaces where we gather. By gathering, I mean both physically and metaphorically.

With the abovementioned of clouded judgment, I think of a time that my sister was having difficulty making a decision concerning one of her kids. The decision to create ease in a difficult situation, or to let her child learn from a lesson, would benefit them in the long run. She mentioned that sometimes being a mom made it challenging to set boundaries, and undesirable habits from her child persisted. Now, this is not unique to her; it has also happened to many other parents and me. We tend to have clouded judgment and can overlook a situation due to our everlasting love for our children. Eventually, and hopefully, they or we will make the right decision. This same type of clouded judgment can affect us with making decisions with family, friends, romantic partners, coworkers, teammates, neighbors, and any human interaction we have. In situations where you feel you have clouded judgment, I suggest you seek the counsel of a sibling, another parent, a friend, a confidant, and in some cases, a professional. Someone that can be a sounding board to help you make the decision that you more than likely instinctively already knew was the right decision.

Sometimes, it isn't just clouded judgment holding us back; sometimes, it's fear. Often, we let fear get in the way, but allowing fear to hold us back isn't the way to do things. As mentioned in the *Gift of Fear* by Gavin de Becker, he states that "intuition is always right in at least two important ways; It is always in response to something. It always has your best interest at heart." For me, fear is a catalyst for change. Suppose a personal relationship has me feeling fearful. In that case, it informs me that something is wrong or right and that I need to make a decision. You might be wondering why I said wrong or right; sometimes, fear can be in taking the next step towards deepening the relationship or bond, such as getting married, which would make it a good thing, the right thing, and vice versa if it is wrong, you've been too afraid to make the decision to move on.

When detaching from a relationship, a song that comes to mind is *This Feeling* by the Chainsmokers, where the lyrics state, "They tell me to think with my head, not that thing in my chest," which I believe that most of us can relate to, we often lead with our heart, when sometimes we have to think with our brain. In cases of family in friends, we have to find balance; to do so, you'll need to trust both your brain and your heart. Intuitively and sometimes with a bit of encouragement from someone who might see the big picture, you'll know what to do when the timing is right.

Additionally Marie Kondo's "Does this spark joy?", can be applied to family and friends. Do your relationships bring you joy? If not you might want to reevaluate those relationships, but this is definitely a double-edge sword as some friends "spark joy," but can be bad for us.

Bonus: I know that this chapter has been all about disruption, dismantling and detaching. But how do some builds/acquisitions happen where we may want to dismantle? Not everything needs to be dismantled and acquiring can be a good thing.

For instance, I remember my first apartment and the reality that it presented. When I was younger and would argue with my mom about running away or moving out, she'd laugh and shake her head. During this particular argument, I told her I'd move to a studio apartment far away and have all the space I needed. My mom laughed as she often did and said that I had no idea what a studio apartment was; she said it'd be so small and that I would have no space, that I'd be sleeping next to my stove and fridge. As a young artist, I thought that a studio apartment was like the big spacious lofts I had seen in 80's films, and boy was I wrong. But in all honesty, when I look back at all my favorite spaces that I called home, it was my first studio apartment and those smaller spaces. I didn't have much with my first studio apartment and slowly built on creating a home.

Limited space meant I didn't need much and limited my quest to acquire more. As life changed and my home requirements needed to match my lifestyle, I acquired more material possessions over the years. It was not a bad thing, as when my children lived with me, it was a three-person home. I fondly remember my ex visiting from New York City for the first time and finding comfort in the home I created. When parting after a long weekend, he looked me in the eyes and said, "Rico, you've created a home here; it's really a home." Hearing this confirmed that I had successfully created a home for my kids and me. I understood what he meant, as he had something similar with two roommates, but I had a home and a family, and my two-bedroom apartment reflected that. As I age and consider my options of where I'll live should I ever be solo again, I'd happily return to that first studio apartment or home I shared with my kids.

Chapter Five - Accountability

My friend "LAUREN," you might wonder why I put Lauren in all caps and quotes. For me, it's because she is the embodiment of accountability and has further taught me the importance of accountability.

Accountability can play a key role in how successful of a start or consistent you are in implementing change. I had already learned the effectiveness of accountability through my running group. Initially, when I started running, I joined a local run-walk program, a Galloway running group; two of my coworkers had signed up for the *Chicago Marathon*, and since I enjoyed dashing across a field while playing softball, I figured I had what it takes to complete the marathon (I didn't say "a marathon" specifically, because in Chicago there is "the Marathon" as we all refer to it). Of course, I'm not entirely delusional; playing softball does not equal being able to run a marathon, but being accountable and showing up for weekend runs, especially the long runs, does. Joining a running group was the best thing I've ever done. Many people in my pace group held me accountable to be there on time to do the weekday runs and be prepared for the weekend runs.

Although I can tell you tons of stories about my running career, I want to share the story about me and my friend Lauren. You might remember me mentioning Lauren in the first chapter; she's the one that got me to take my first spin class. As we often did on our way to our medical association job, we often had conversations about relationships, home life, and career hopes. Not that we weren't delighted with our careers, but we both inherently knew that one must continue to grow and develop new skills in all facets of work and life. In a very "can you keep a secret" conversation, Lauren expressed her interest in moving to Dubai and furthering her communication and marketing career. I secretly shared that I wanted to become a spin instructor. For her, it would be a life-altering event, where she would leave the comfort of Chicago to pursue her dream, and little did I know that for me, what I thought would be a supplement to my existence would prove to be a life-changing event as well. I don't recall what day it was that we made the pact and challenged each other. Still, I remember telling Lauren that I would become a spin instructor if she went for it and made Dubai happen. Sometime after, Lauren had some very early morning interviews right after spin as it was the afternoon in Dubai, landed a job, and thus began my pursuit of becoming a spin instructor and holding up my part of the pact. At about the same time that Lauren moved to Dubai, I became a spin instructor. This story is accountability to the MAX. Once again, I have to say, if we can do it, so can you!

Like the story above, I have come to realize that accountability is essential to success. Sometimes, it comes down to whether it's extrinsic or intrinsic. For me, accountability to a friend, work, or goal is a nice push, but what I've found and what's incredible is the accountability I have for myself. A common thread among my life achievements is the goals and expectations I have set for myself and how I have held myself accountable. When I set these goals, I share them and automatically create the framework for accountability. There is not one goal out there that I have kept to myself; at some point or another, I shout it out to the universe, and thus the process begins. This commonality has presented itself when I told myself I would be a spin instructor, parent, yoga teacher, runner, educator, team leader, coach, etcetera. My accountability and goals list seem endless, and sometimes I have to simmer with it before I bring it to fruition, just like in cooking, where marinating helps to infuse the flavor needed for a well-spiced meal, marinating on an idea for a bit assures that it's going to have all the spice it needs. Think about it and play *Spice Up Your Life* by the Spice Girls.

Bonus: Recognizing that accountability can be a curse or a blessing. Accountability is that angel or devil on your shoulder, and human nature has a way of making us accountable regardless of what it may be. Accountability comes in the form of good or bad habits, an employer, a friend, a family member, or a group fitness class. Who and how you choose to be accountable is up to you. For example, sometimes, accountability can come in the form of a negative remark; when I became a single parent to my brother's children, I specifically remember being told that as a single man, I wouldn't be able to do it. This remark itself fueled the fire within me and created an accountable measure based on a negative remark. Another example I'd like to share is that sometimes we're being accountable without realizing how much so. I have a friend who loves to take photos and has gotten into the habit of taking pictures on her walk to the train for work and posting these photos on Instagram.

The photos vary, from springtime flowers to snowcapped iron gates and holiday lights. She had recently started taking pictures of the lake and sending them to our running group text thread every morning. Not only has this become a morning ritual for her, but it has become an expectation for those who are part of our running group. Could my friend possibly feel accountable for posting these photos? If so, I suspect that there will be many more photos coming our way. Accountability can come in many subtle ways, as demonstrated above, or being the one always to host Thanksgiving dinner. Who and what we are accountable to also changes as we mature and our situations change. One day we're accountable to our friends for being out all night partying, with late arrivals to work, or not completing homework assignments (this supports my theory on how some relationships can "spark joy", but can be bad for us). On other days we are accountable for arriving on time and being able to complete tasks.

Chapter Six - Bike Set-Up = Life Set-up

"Mise en place – Putting in Place"

The above is a French term that I've heard. The first time I heard it was in an article from the *Harvard Business Review* website, where they quote Anthony Bourdain, having said in *Kitchen Confidential* that "Mise en place is the religion of all good line cooks." Additionally, the article quotes Bourdain stating that, "As a cook, your station, and its condition, its state of readiness, is an extension of your nervous system," he continues. "The Universe is in order when your station is set up the way you like it: you know where to find everything with your eyes closed, everything you need during the course of the shift is at the ready at arm's reach, your defenses are deployed." In the same article, author Ron Friedman is quoted as saying "What's the first thing you do when you arrive at your desk? For many of us, checking email or listening to voice mail is practically automatic. In many ways these are among the worst ways to start a day. Both activities hijack our focus and put us in a reactive mode, where other people's priorities take center stage. They are the equivalent of entering a kitchen and looking for a spill to clean or a pot to scrub."

The importance of the above two quotes needs to be taken to heart. For me, the importance of setting up a playlist that will motivate and challenge riders is integral to a great ride. The playlist also becomes an extension of my cueing, my physical manifestation while I am on the bike, and leads me not blindly but with each beat and lyric. When thinking about bike set-up, a rider must ensure that their bike set-up is to their specifications, recognizing that bike set-up can make for a good or bad ride. Seat and handlebar height is essential in setting you up for comfort and alignment for better form and enjoyment and protecting your knees from undue stress. Like Bourdain, I like setting up a clean, organized space. A clean, prepared space helps you tackle the task at hand. Bourdain, once in an interview, stated that before cooking, he gathered all of the recipe ingredients, utensils, and pots and pans that he would need to start cooking. Imagine that your desk is an elaborate recipe, and the final product is a super yummy outcome. Most recipes appear to be challenging, but when you have all the ingredients in place, you realize that the recipe itself is basic. Today, we have the luxury of many tools to help us get our jobs done, but even these tools can be overwhelming or unnecessary.

For your at office set-up, I recommend sticking to the basics and keeping a clean desk and computer icon desktop. In reality, you only need a pad of paper, your computer, a mouse, a wireless keyboard, and as many screens as possible to do your job efficiently. But as I mentioned earlier, I trained myself to work efficiently with the laptop keyboard, hence not needing that wireless one I purchased from Amazon. The only electronics on my desk are those mentioned above and a beautiful lamp with the base of a silver tree and faux bird (the lamp inspires me and gives me something to look at). I recommend keeping all other electronics, like cell phones, tablets, and other distractors, in another room or on a counter away from your desk and, in addition to this, turning off or muting notifications that ding on your computer when you get a new email or message.

The same goes for your physical workspace furnishings; traditionally, our workspaces were designed by interior designers or office engineers based on the demands of our jobs. For some, it might be a simple computer, monitor, and telephone setup. For others, there may be multiple monitors and varied lighting. With others in close proximity via a cubicle or office space, allowing us access to them when there is a need for a conversation or just due to limited office space. As many of us are now working from home, we have been tasked with creating the perfect work environment. For me my director job requires that I have at least three computer screens, but I opt for one large monitor attached to the wall and the screen attached to my laptop.

I like simplicity in both my home and my setup. I still have a third monitor, though; this one I keep upstairs in the living room for when I want a change of scenery. In addition to the lamp, I also have a plant to nurture, a pen holder, a notepad, and a frame with a picture of my kids and grandson. Even this setup can get disrupted with mail, vitamins, coffee cups, and water bottles. Most folks would be comfortable and productive with this setup, but you have to do what works for you. Take a look at your desk setup and simply remove anything that doesn't contribute to your workday. I toyed back and forth on whether to put the word simply in the above sentence, but really it is that simple. Instead of selecting what should go, you should ask yourself what is needed to get the job done. Only keep what is required, and then add a memento or something that inspires you.

For me, it's the picture of my kids and grandson and the plant to remind me that life exists and is forever changing. The setup is the most important part of your workflow; just like in a spin class, proper alignment sets the stage for efficiency. Additionally, like in spin class, your riding posture is critical for a safe, enjoyable ride, and your chair and desk should be ergonomically sound to meet your specific height and grasp needs.

So, grab your towel and get to sweating; here comes your ride.

Set-up at home, I follow a minimalist way of doing things; in my kitchen, there is limited stuff on the counter, usually, only things that are often in use. For example, we have a Keurig at home, and every night I fill the Keurig with water. The coffee pods are conveniently kept in a pod drawer under the Keurig, making it easy for me to have my morning coffee routine. The little pod drawer was a pleasant surprise because when my partner first purchased it, I was like, "oh, here we go again," another useless product that is just going to clutter our kitchen counter but, in reality, has added value to my routine and my day. I'll chat more about this in a later chapter when we get to decluttering.

Regarding the warm-up for home organization, you'll want to start by making a list of what you have in a particular room; you'll need one list for each room. For example, I use this list exercise when I work one-on-

one with personal training clients or friends who want to begin working out. I start by asking them what they have regarding space and fitness equipment. Some spew the same response, a treadmill, old dumbbells, a yoga mat; some state a total body workout machine, and most respond with the fact that they've only used it once.

Some mention that the building they live in has a fitness room and list all the fitness room equipment.

Next, I ask them to draw the fitness room or area; this will give them and me a better understanding of what is available to them and what workouts can be implemented within the space. When organizing your home, you start with the warm-up, listing everything you own, preferably with the big items.

— Preferably you'll break it down like this:
— Livingroom – Sofa, coffee table, two seating chairs, entertainment center, side tables.
— Kitchen – Table, five chairs, microwave, toaster, toaster oven, mixer.
— Bedroom – Bed, two nightstands, carpet, dresser, armoire, standup mirror.
— Dining Room – Dining table, buffet, six chairs, rolling bar cart.
— Extra Room - (home office, workout room, crafting room), whatever it may be list all items.

Once you have listed all the items, you can work on removing and setting up your space.

Set-up for family, friends, and relationships. Most of us have heard the term chosen family, and now is an excellent time to recognize and present that term. In the web article *What "Chosen Family' Means – and how to Build Your Own* Gabrielle Kassel quotes Bahiyyah Maroon as saying that "a chosen family is made up of people who have intentionally chosen to embrace, nurture, love, and support each other regardless of blood or marriage." Now's the time to set up your life and keep relationships that add value to your life and remove toxic people from your life. Just as you set the stage for your work and home, the same goes for setting the stage for the relationships you keep. However, as with work and life, we can't omit all situations, but we can limit our interactions with others.

With all three above, I want you to think of two examples. While obtaining my personal training certification, I learned that if you're at a workout facility and there is a damaged, broken, or malfunctioning piece of equipment, you remove it from the area, you don't put a sign on it that says out of order, because a patron can easily remove that sign. You remove the broken equipment and only return it when it is repaired. In relationship situations, if you can't repair the relationship or item in your home, remove it. The second example is the one that is happening to me right now; I am at a coffee shop and sitting on the coolest antique chair; however, whenever I move or get up, my jeans snag on a decorative nail head sticking out of the chair. Eventually, I will have to go to the counter and inform the staff of the chair before I leave so that they can remove it and it does not snag or damage someone's clothing; this simple task has created efficiency and a safe environment. If something snags your day, remove it.

Bonus: Regarding proper set-up. I have knitted and crocheted many baby blankets in my years of fiber arts. In doing so, I found that after a brief review of the likes or themes the parents have chosen for their baby's nesting spot, I can easily develop an idea that will shine through and give me direction in creating a baby blanket that they and their new bundle of joy would cherish for years to come. For example, I've included a baby blanket photo at the end of this book. It's farmed-themed and all so cute for a young mind, with corn that's soft to the touch, a horse's mane for playtime, a silo, a widdle pig, and a red barn house. The blanket was an idea I had in mind and although I didn't have an opportunity to consult with the parents, I created something that I believe that they too could enjoy. The blanket itself serves two purposes; the first is that it has held me accountable for delivering on my promise to provide a handmade gift. The second, with its textures and vibrant colors, serves as a functional item for the kid. The photo of the baby on the back of the book is the icing on the cake.

Chapter Seven - Components of a Ride

For the components of a ride, you'll notice that I have broken down each component further into three categories, Work, Home, and Personal (Family & Friends); in some cases, work has been broken down further into work within the office and work from home. Please note that terminology in spin classes changes within the different providers of spin class instruction; the following components are generally used, as well as concepts such as "in-the-saddle."

Warm-Up

In a spin class the Warm-up is the time where you prepare for the ride ahead, the resistance on the bike prepares you for the ride you are about to endure.

The Warm-Up should be a time when you anticipate your needs for your workday, your home, and your relationships. The set-up leads directly into the warm-up.

When thinking of warming up, you'll have to consider what is required to get moving. For work, some needs are seasonal, such as a yearly cyclic event, for example, a membership renewal phase, where the whole team works together to renew members. For home, it can be spring cleaning or setting up your space for the holidays! A warm-up for personal relationships could be birthdays, holidays, and milestones. For example, if your child moves away to college, your home life changes, as well as your everyday relationships with those around you and your child. The relationship with your child will change as they gain more independence; it will be an adjustment for the two of you. These types of changes can affect your wallet and impact whether you get that sewing or fitness room you've always wanted. Depending on the situation, you'll need to warm up in all three components. Most importantly, before we get into separating work, home, and personal, your day should start with a walk, yoga, workout, morning coffee, reading, or anything that sets the tone for the day.

Work Warm-Up

Use this time to set the tone for the day. As mentioned earlier, you should have everything in its place, and now it's time for you to determine what needs to be done. Many experts recommended creating a "to-do" list the day before of what you would like to accomplish the next day. For me, it's laying out my workout clothes and spin shoes the night before. But I will loop back to this in the strong finisher component of the ride, essentially your day. But for now, if you are going to reference this list, you'll use this list to set the tone for the day. As mentioned earlier in the Bike Set-up chapter, author Ron Friedman advises not to look at email.

However, I recommend that you look at emails with a different mindset, the mindset to clear out clutter and not respond to the email's content immediately. But to determine if anything takes priority over some of the tasks you hope to accomplish for the day, determine any emails that can be immediately removed from your email inbox.

My process usually goes like this, delete, delete, delete; I remove all spam email (and most importantly, set up the email function to identify emails as spam so that it goes immediately into my junk folder) by deleting my spam email, it gives me a sense of immediate accomplishment, next I quickly review remaining emails for information, information comes in two types of emails, one is the solely informational email, followed by emails that require a bit more time or a response. Usually, with a quick glance at the informational email, you can quickly move it to its respective folder, where emails that require a bit more time can be left in the inbox to review and follow up with later. Any other follow-up emails can be placed on your "to-do" list to be strategic about where you put the email on the list. Only some things are priorities.

With the abovementioned spam email, I've noticed that no matter how much we try to block spam mail, we still receive it; in today's technological and data-driven world, it is easy to find ourselves on lists. There are people and algorithms whose sole purpose is to find and add us to listservs; we must be diligent in our quest to block these junk emails and unsubscribe from said lists.

Now for a little bit of music, *I Gotta Feeling* by the Black-Eyed Peas lyrics "I've gotta feeling that tonight's gonna be a good night" is a great song to start your day. You need to exchange the word "tonight" with "today" and at the end of the sentence "night" with "day," for example, "I've gotta feeling that today's gonna be a good day ."This song will have you smash it! Not only that, but this song also cleverly says the days of the week and helps us move through the days with ease! It's a celebratory song that gets you moving—urging you to do it again. This song is also great for a hill climb in spin class.

Home Warm-Up

At home, the warm-up is just as important; as mentioned above, I have a way of laying out my clothes for my early morning fitness classes. Well, your home is the same; in many ways, these two warm-ups are the same and contribute to each other. When preparing to make changes in your home, the warm-up should include a quick observation of what state your home currently is in, not state as in where you live, but the overall flow, appearance, and furnishings inside your home. Ok, the state was like a dad joke; bear with me; a little humor goes a long way.

After you have determined your home's state, you'll need to visualize what you would like your home to be. Usually, your home should be conducive to your lifestyle. For me, it's having a tranquil retreat, which allows for creativity, workouts, and, believe it or not, a bit of chaos. I know that chaos doesn't go with the other descriptors I mentioned, but chaos can play an important role in disrupting and keeping us on our toes. Once you know what you would like your home to be, you have done your warm-up and are ready for the next steps.

In addition to the above exercise, looking for ways to rethink your space can be found on realtor websites such as Redfin or Zillow. When I sold my first condo, my realtor suggested how to clean up the space and prepare for photos and an open house. The process required removing most personal items, such as family photos and art that may not be to everyone's liking, eliminating clutter on countertops, putting some furniture in storage, and moving furniture around to create flow. At first, I was disturbed by the idea of removing family photos and making these changes because, in my mind, I thought that family photos and a lived-in home would assist the buyer in envisioning their own family calling this place their home. In reality, a minimalist clean slate helps the buyer to visualize their own furnishings and family photos occupying the home. During this exercise of envisioning your retreat, it's a good idea to do something similar when designing your home, taking out not the family photos but taking away pieces of furniture and getting your place to open house simplicity. This newly added freedom of less suits you, and you'll be more inclined to keep it that way.

Personal (Family & Friends) Warm-Up

For warm-ups pertaining to your relationships, I want to share a quote that I recently heard on Simon Sinek's podcast *A Bit of Optimism*; in an episode with Maria Shriver during the COVID-19 pandemic, where the two of them were on a walk outside, Shriver picked up a phone call from one of her children.

Shriver mentions to Sinek that she contemplated picking up the phone call and told Sinek that she always picks up a call from her children so that they always know that no matter what the situation or what the call is about, she will pick up the phone and that they were her priority. With this, I understood that Maria Shriver's approach is very similar to how I meet the demands of my children, family, partner, and friends, recognizing that they are a priority and deserving of my attention. Although some of them take precedence over others, through my actions, I hope that they know that they are all important to me. Identifying who my priorities are is the warm-up in my relationships.

Bonus: A warm-up can occur the night before; for example, when a couple is ready to tie the knot, usually the day before the wedding, there is a rehearsal dinner or wedding rehearsal. Essentially, in all that you do, a little bit of preparation or rehearsal can set you up for success so that you can jump right in the next day.

I always warm up for a class by riding through my playlist on my stationary bike at home. I also recall warm-ups for work situations; for example, when I have held meetings at a hotel, I would meet with the hotel staff the day before to review meeting set-up, food and beverages, registration area if needed, and to ensure that meeting specifications have been met. This way, the following day, I can hit the floor running. Additionally, in the meeting example, the warm-up can also happen months before when you are on-site inspecting the hotel, negotiating the contract, and figuring out meeting logistics.

In any case, warm-ups can apply to your regular workdays; sometimes, we get to the office or turn on our computers and must immediately get to work, jumping right in!

Break

"When everything is goin' wrong
Don't worry, it won't last for long
Yeah, it's all gonna come around
Don't let it get you down
You gotta keep on holding on"
Up - Shania Twain

Stop reading this book and go listen to this song. Sometimes, we feel overwhelmed, that life challenges are tearing us down, and that we are about to lose it. In Shania's lyrics, she sings about forgetting to fill up on gas. Besides being a literal translation of forgetting something so simple, in reality, we do get so busy that we sometimes forget to fill up on gas. So, it makes perfect sense that we need a break from our schedules and life.

A break should be where you replenish your energy, mind, body, and focus. Whether it's meditation, yoga, a meal, or a hobby, you must find something that removes you from the daily cog and allows you to disconnect. Ideally, you should work these breaks into your day. Depending on where I'm teaching, I may work a break into a spin class, but if it isn't the standard at a particular location, I instruct participants that this is their ride and that they should feel free to break when needed.

Now with that being said, I actually do have some form of a break scheduled in my ride; it's not a full-on stop your legs from moving kind of break, but rather an active recovery, a point in a track or within the playlist that occurs after a challenging interval of work, where I slow things down and ask the participants to breathe—essentially catching their breath and bringing them back to a manageable neutral pace. Taking a break while at work is essential to bringing you back to neutral. In this section, I have broken down breaking at work into "actual office" and "work from home" breaks.

Also please note that break shouldn't be singular and that's why you'll see it listed below as "Break(s)."

Break(s) at Work

When breaking at the office, it is essential to get away from your desk and, even more, to get away from your colleagues. For example, in a position I held when I came on board, we were extremely behind in the department's deliverables. As a manager, I felt that I needed to work through lunch and only take a few minutes to gather my lunch quickly or use the bathroom, along with early arrivals and late-night departures from the office, which led to some unhealthy habits. Don't get me wrong, this has been the case in other positions I've held, where overtime was offered, and occasionally working like this seemed necessary, with emphasis on occasionally. By no means should this become a habit. Also, I think it is important for me to mention that my employees were hourly, and their days were structured by call center hours, dictated that they would abide by designated times assigned to them, for arrival, departure, lunch, and breaks, with overtime occasionally mandatory. I say this to demonstrate that my insistence on working through lunch and extra hours wasn't the company's cultural norm.

For me, I prioritized that my employees were taking their breaks and not being overworked during these challenging days.

However, I continued to skip breaks and work long hours, and when looking back, I quickly felt the effects of the stress that accompanied such a schedule. I was tired, I couldn't sleep at night, and my eating habits became unhealthy by choosing quick ready-to-eat meals, which included purchases from vending machines and fast-food restaurants. I noticed that I became extremely moody. Something that isn't a part of my demeanor; usually, I'm relaxed and easygoing. Noticing this change, I quickly turned to an old habit that has helped me to make changes that would be good for me. I signed up for a triathlon. As in previous years, when I made a commitment, I would find the time to hold that commitment. Signing up for the triathlon required me to find time in my day to train, specifically swimming the leg of the triathlon that I was least confident in, so every day at 11:30 AM, I would hit ctrl-alt-delete to lock my computer, and head on over to the local pool to swim some laps. Not only did I notice the changes in my overall demeanor my staff noticed the changes too. I was not mean or irrational in my management, but I believe they noticed that I was less stressed and happier. The work was still there, but things had changed. My outlook changed, and I opted not to work long hours, still finding time to get to the office early because there's a kind of peace at the office when you get there early and no one is there. Emails aren't binging in so frequently, and at the end of the day, I quickly opted to leave the office when most folks left. I began to sleep better, make better nutritional choices, and lead by example. Whatever break you need, you need to find it; whether it's getting away to the coffee shop, a quiet city park, or a cafeteria, you must take that break and breathe or, in my case, swim.   In addition to the above, I enhanced my meditation practice to include moments of meditation throughout my workday.

Break(s) When Working at Home

When breaking from work at home, the lines of when a break should occur can become blurred. Although the scenario in the above example of working long hours is not ideal, it was apparent when the work day ended and when one should go home. Workdays in the office usually have a clear start and end point, and these clear start and end times create a steadfast pause from your workday. As mentioned earlier, when the COVID-19 pandemic hit, many of us started to work from home, and although today, many have returned to their physical office spaces, many are still working from home and, in some cases, are now full-on remote employees. At home, the lines between home life and work life become blurred; we can easily get caught up in the workday and skip necessary breaks and lunches. Finding ourselves drinking tons of coffee and eating meals at our desks, you'll notice I said meals because, besides lunch, we're also eating breakfast and dinner at our desks. When working from home, getting your breaks in is much more critical.

Whether you clock in or out, yes, some folks must still do that, especially with retail or call center work, where employees' schedules are dependent on having coverage to serve their customer base. However, there is no actual clock in or out for the work I do, and sometimes I wish there was because it would automatically dictate that I take a break. But in this case, designing your day to include breaks and a solid beginning and an end is essential to your workday playlist. When I started working from home, I enjoyed the benefit of no commute and the benefits of being able to wake up, turn my computer on and have access to work 24 hours a day, and I mean just that. I am most creative and energized during the early morning. Although my assigned, chosen schedule dictated that I start work at 7:30 AM, I found that if I couldn't sleep, I'd wake up, log in, and begin work.

In some cases, I'd log in as early as 4:30 AM; this was a bit due to the fact that on some days, I'd teach early morning fitness classes which required me to be up at 5:00 AM and at the gym ready to instruct at 6:00 AM. My body is programmed to rise early, and with trying to keep my body's clock in tune, I opted always to be a part of the 5:00 AM Club. For me, waking up earlier some days and later other days wreaked havoc on my body and its circadian rhythm. It also confused my dogs, who depended on my schedule for their walks and feeding times. I'm pretty sure that the same applies to most people.

When I was first tasked with working from home, it allowed me to identify and create new morning routines that set the tone for the day. Usually, my day began with a meditation, possibly yoga, the workouts I instructed, or a shower. Yes, I must mention showers because, as we all know, when we started working from home, showers weren't always first on our list; most of us found ourselves wearing pajama pants and presentable shirts on top. Unlike having to go to a physical office space didn't have a morning routine that dictated we be presentable and out the door at a specific time. Working from home also removed that valuable commuting time, where I often found relaxation in a good book or a knitting project I was working on. Since working from home directly relates to your home life playlist, I'll provide more break information in the following passage. Note that you must have clear lines drawn to separate your home and work life when working from home. I had to draw some hardlines of when I worked; even though I enjoyed logging in earlier, I forced myself not to turn my work computer on until 7:30 AM, I physically walked away from my desk for meals, and at the end of the day, I quickly shut down my computer and the energy source to it which was a power strip that also had my desk lamp connected to it, so that when I shut down the energy source, the room went dark. I also flipped over my notepad and left the room. It's as easy as that, no complicated end-of-work-day routines. Just shut it down.

Break(s) at Home

When thinking about breaks at home, it should be synonymous with "retreat," a break within a retreat, finding your space from your family, roommates, friends, noise, and pets. Before I worked from home, I used to dream about what it would be like; I'd start and end my day at the same time each day, prepare and eat fresh meals, and zip through my days with ease. Well, let's say that my dream wasn't at all my reality; I had underestimated just how much work would be required to make that dream happen and how much attention the inhabitants of my home would require. For example, my dogs wanted all my attention, 24/7, from sleeping on my bed to sitting at the shower's glass door to finding a cozy spot next to my feet while I worked. Their quest for my attention was unsurpassed. I had to learn quickly about opportunities to enhance their walking schedule and create space for them to live within my workspace. For example, I purchased a dog bed that allowed them to snooze next to my desk. Creating these opportunities and space for them helped me not feel guilty when blocking them out of my office space. Your work-from-home workday allows you to create breaks that can also accomplish some things. For example, my boss and I recently implemented the 100 push-ups a day challenge for thirty days, for which I set a timer every thirty minutes to get off my chair and do 25 push-ups. Not only was this challenge fun, but it also got me away from my desk and allowed me to renew my focus and strengthen my muscles. A task like this worked for me. What might work for you?

As you create your spaces at home, choose colors, art, and furnishings that motivate you and allow you to relax. For example, if your retreat involves your yoga practice, choose mats, blocks, and bands that soothe and inspire you. It might seem like it wouldn't make a big difference, but I'm definitely motivated by the design and colors of my Les Mills equipment. Whatever your break involves, be sure that anything associated with taking a break is pleasing.

Breaks Personal (Family & Friends)

Creating breaks in your relationships equals time away and distance to have time for yourself. The demands imposed by family and friends can be emotionally and time-consuming. It is important to set expectations by regularly letting folks know that you value your alone time and that although they are a priority, other things require your time, including doing nothing. In Michelle Obama's book *Becoming*, Mrs. Obama states, "It's ok to flip these priorities and to only care for ourselves once in awhile ." I'm sure that Mrs. Obama's role as mother and wife to one of our past presidents required that she meet their needs and meet the expectations it took to be First Lady of the United States. I'm sure that she had to learn to balance the expectations of family, close friends, and the public. Her statement alone informs us that to be well and find balance in the world we live in; we must remove ourselves from the demands of family and find balance by putting ourselves first. Even if it is for a short amount of time, her example and statement reflect that no matter your role, you must make time for YOU. There's a Chicago House music song called Break for Love by Raze that reminds me to find time in my day to break for love, to break for us, to break for finding balance; in a sense, breaking for love means finding time for yourself. When we love ourselves, we can love others.

Hill - Climb

There are two types of Climbs or Hills: the out-of-the-saddle climb and the in-the-saddle climb. Both are difficult and provide significant benefits in strengthening your muscles and endurance.

Work Hill - Climb

In the Saddle Climb – In Brian Tracey's book *Eat that Frog*, I have found that his advice aligns with my thoughts on how to approach completing an unwanted or difficult, challenging task. Tracey suggests "eating your biggest frog first," stating that "it is the most disgusting, ugliest frog of the bunch ." In spin class, that frog would be the in the saddle climb, where you turn up the resistance and push through until the interval or music track is completed. You'll apply that same concept here; you gather all you need to complete the task and do not end until the task is completed. Completing this challenging task first gives you an opportunity to find success early in your day and not only gives you a sense of relief that the task is now behind you and frees up your mind to focus on other projects. Depending on the task, there usually isn't a set time-limited. You'll find that the time it takes to complete the task may surprise you and only take 20-30 minutes, or it'll live up to its unattractiveness and take one, two, or more hours. A climb at work should strengthen your mind and skillset. You'll build confidence and endurance in preparation for a similar challenge with another similar task. You'll notice the difference, just as I do in my cycling classes, in class I can see the work of the riders pushing through increased resistance and the noticeable sigh of relief that comes after a climb, and knowing that the next time they are challenged with that resistance, that they will approach it and conquer it again and again.

Out of Saddle Climb - This is where you test the waters; you jump right in and start to tackle the quick "to-dos" on your list. Please keep in mind that each of these shouldn't take more than 15-20 minutes, allowing you to complete at least three tasks within an hour. You can also use this time to do standard process stuff that seems mindless and doesn't vary in demand. For example, reviewing data for accuracy, updating client records, meeting preparation, and following up with any low-hanging fruit.

Home Hill - Climb

A climb at home should make things easier, whether it's clean-up, reorganizing a cluttered drawer, or dusting. It also might be a great time to eliminate no longer wanted or used items.

In the Saddle climb – If you're like me, the climb might be cleaning the stove, bathroom, and closets or cleaning out and scrubbing the inside of the fridge. It is usually a task you aren't excited about but needs to be done. If this is the case, it's a great time to get out that heavy metal album that your mom wouldn't let you listen to and play it loud. But remember, be sure you have everything you need to get the job done so that you're not interrupted by trying to find extra cleaning agents, latex gloves, or scrub pads. You'll definitely need the warm-up for this task.

Out of saddle climb – Using the example above of the stove, bathroom, or fridge, you can also dedicate only 20 minutes to the chore by just cleaning out the fridge of leftovers and expired products, wiping down the stove to get any food crumbs or spices off, and in your bathroom doing a quick refresh, like taking a brush to the toilet bowl.

Considering the above two climbs, I think about an article by Shifrah Combiths titled *The 20-Minute Daily Routine That'll Give You Your Weekends Back*, where Combiths advises, "To get to your housework to-dos before the weekend, commit to cleaning for 15 to 20 minutes five days a week." Combiths further breaks it down into two categories "one that you repeat everyday as a matter of habit and ones that you do once a week." The above ideas presented by Combiths go perfectly with my idea of two different types of climbs for your home, the first in the saddle climb would be the chores you do once or twice a week, and the daily habit of cleaning closely resembles an out of saddle climb.

Family and Friends Hill - Climb

A climb with family and friends should strengthen the relationship. Sometimes, something is getting to you, egging you on, something that you are discontent with, and you're going to have to lean into it head-on. Resentment is a beast and can fester quickly or slowly build up until an all-out explosion occurs. An explosion where words are said and feelings are hurt. Understanding how you feel about something is critical in supporting why it may be unnerving; additionally, understanding how your partner or family member may feel about something is necessary for overcoming challenges and strife.

In the Saddle Climb - Beyonce said it best! "To the left, to the left, everything you own in the box to the left." Some changes are tough and require you to permanently cut off someone to live a better life and remove toxicity. "Baby, your Toxic," Britney Spears. Additionally, some relationships have run their course, and it's time to let go. Allow yourself some time to plan how you will let this person or persons go and then do it, "Eat that Frog." Please note that this is the first step and that you'll have to allow yourself some time to mourn this loss because it will feel like a loss and then will eventually feel like freedom. Freedom from whatever strife holding onto that relationship played in your life—such as unwarranted stress, having to be the one to initiate hangouts, maintaining the relationship, and dealing with the toxicity that accompanied that relationship. Sometimes this may require baby steps, and that's why I chose to assign this kind of task as one that mimics a climb. Climbs are supposed to be tough, but we're stronger for having done it in the end. In spin class, when you're in the saddle, fewer muscles are being used to propel you forward as opposed to being out of the saddle, where more muscles are engaged.

Out of Saddle Climb – This is more based on making changes you can take in stride. On the surface, you'll like to create more time for yourself, but out of habit, you tend to fill up your white space with personal and other obligations. You may remember me mentioning this in the Interval component of the ride. To dive deeper, I'd like to share s statement by Nicole Blake Johnson where she says to "Block time off on your calendar for deep work or creative thinking." Johnson's quote is about work, but this can be applied to all facets of your life. For family and friends, I recommend starting to prioritize those relationships that are important to you and stopping saying yes to those that aren't as important. It can be as simple as creating a list. A great practice exercise would be to imagine that you are making your wedding guest list. You sit down and write down everyone you think you would like to attend, and then realize that you have a limited budget and will have to narrow down the list. You'll learn quickly to be cutthroat and strikethrough those that aren't so important to be at your wedding, as Anthony Marentino, in a *Sex and the City* episode, exclaimed, "Cutthroat. I love it. I hope you're this decisive when it comes to location and the dress."

Finding time for those important to you won't be the only way to use your white space; you'll also need to keep that white space open for alone time when you can replenish and do things solely for yourself. Fill the whitespace with a simple title of "me time." Keeping the above in mind won't be the only way to protect your white space; you need to take it a step further and only say yes if you don't already have an existing family or friend commitment that week.

Abiding by this one commitment to a family member rule is important because saying yes to a second commitment within a week is exactly how white space gets eaten up.

Before you know it, you have two to three weekly commitments that will consume your whole month. Identifiable boundaries, like only saying yes if you don't already have an obligation, are crucial to keeping your white space open.

Stay determined in this endeavor as you would do a real climb in a spin class step by step. Each pedal stroke gets you closer to your desired goal — finish the climb strong!

Dash – Race – Speed - Sprint

In spin class, you'll find that there is an opportunity to lighten the resistance and pick up the speed. But believe me, less resistance does not equal ease; it will still take effort to pick up the pace and move through the song. Usually, speed is one on a flat road in the saddle. One of my certifications is in Les Mills' Sprint, a class that embodies speed intervals and moves you through increased RPMs, which closely resembles what you would do in a spin class. When creating my spin class playlist, each track must match the level of work required to complete the component. For a race, I usually select an upbeat and fun song, usually a dance song from 110 to 130 BPMs, to match the RPM criteria and allow the rider to let the music move them. This ride component can occur a couple of tracks after the warm-up, during the middle, or at the end of your ride. In any case, at least three dashes, races, or speed help to vary the ride and increase a rider's endurance. In addition to speed intervals being placed throughout the ride, I always like a dash at the end to help us finish strong, breathless, drenched in sweat, and adrenaline pumping. Allowing the cooldown to be much more noticeable with breathwork, stretches, and celebratory words to match the work we've just done. As you develop your playlist and know your workday requirements, your home life, and your family and friends, you'll be able to apply a dash track anywhere needed. Some tracks that are good for this are Timmy Trumpets *Oracle*, and Johnny Vicious' radio mix of Whitney Houston's *I Look to You*.

Work Dash – Race – Speed - Sprint

For your workday, this is where you look at the clock and realize that you're approaching your half-day mark, or end of the day, and that now is a good time to respond to some of those emails.

Think of it in terms of Tina Turner's *Proud Mary*, where the "Big wheels keep on turning" and "Proud Mary keeps on Burnin." You'll want to zip through those emails, allowing yourself at least half an hour to clean out any new emails, flush out the junk, and head out to lunch or home. Similar to a spin class, you'll determine when is a good time to pop in a speed interval; this is your ride; you can go as fast or slow as you'd like, and you can switch it up as needed.

Home Dash-Race-Speed - Sprint

Mad dash at home is the quick pick-up, the quick I need to get this done now.

You can do this one of two ways: a grand sweep of your whole home or tackle one room at a time. A grand sweep of your home means you go from room to room. For example, I grab a laundry basket or a handy boxed-shaped reusable grocery bag to pick up clutter. It goes something like this; I'm in my living room. I pick up leftover mail, socks, shoes, games, books, and dog toys, and if it belongs in that room, I put it in its proper place, and then everything else goes into the basket. Trash and recyclables go into their respective bin, and I run a wet disinfectant wipe on all surfaces. What is left in the laundry basket gets a tour of the house, finding its way into its assigned location, not on a countertop or chair in its designated area, but in the actual place, it should go. Keeping in mind accessibility, for example, games and books are often in rotation. They are usually housed on a shelf that is easy to get to and in a room where they are most frequently used. This idea is a carryover from the proper set-up component when organizing your home. I do the above in every room; you'd be surprised how many living room items make it into the bedroom, or when my kids were young, I'd find plates and cups in their bedroom.

Finding the time to clean up can be a challenge in itself. When my kids were younger, cleaning up was something that I did at the end of the night while they were preparing for bed and showering.

During this nighttime ritual, I'd pick up every out-of-place item and quickly identify items that needed to go into their bedroom and place them there. Then as they were venturing to dreamland, I'd complete the process in the other rooms of our home. As mentioned earlier, my mom would play her records loudly, which signaled to us kids that it was the weekend and we were to get up and have breakfast and help with the weekend chores; this wasn't just your regular clean-up but a deep clean of the house. We'd organize our clothes for laundry, sweep and mop the floors, and wipe down walls with a concoction of dish soap, bleach, and water. It wasn't fun for us kids because we'd much rather be out playing. Still, the music definitely helped to motivate us and let us connect with our mom in a way that wouldn't have happened if she didn't create this routine—allowing us to both appreciate her music and all the work it took to maintain a home.

When I think of the music played in my childhood home, I consider myself lucky because my parents had an eclectic taste for music, including a combination of Motown beats, country music, Elvis, the Beatles, and big-band Mexican music.

Not only is timing important when completing a task at home, but so is the choice of music; for instance, around the holidays, Christmas for example, Christmas-themed music is usually on when putting up a tree and decorating the house. Bing, Bing, another way music plays a big part in our lives and traditions. What's your home clean-up music? What music comes to mind when wanting to get something done quickly?

Personal (Family & Friends) Dash-Race-Speed - Sprint

I want you to think about Run DMC's lyrics, "it's like that, and that's the way it is" sometimes accepting what is, is the best way to address an issue or concern. You might be behind on paying bills and continue to rack up more debt. Not accepting your situation will only lead to increased debt and eventually dealing with creditors, poor credit, and overall anxiety about your situation.

Addressing your financial situation head-on will help you to strategize and develop a plan. Another example is holding onto a toxic relationship that no longer serves you. Keeping in line with Run DMC's lyrics above, accepting what is, will be the start of leading you in the right direction of leaving the relationship or seeking therapy or assistance from others in finding the courage to go or salvage the relationship. "It's like that, and that's the way it is."   In situations where you have to accept what is, you'll want to jump right in like you're racing in a spin class and take action to make the needed changes. This concept is a mad dash to get the task done.

Jog

"At first I was afraid I was petrified, thinking I could never live without you by my side, but then I spent so many nights feeling sorry for myself and I grew strong, I learned how to get along," *I Will Survive* - Gloria Gaynor.

During the marathon training season, I run at least two to three times a week; ideally, a week of runs is two short weekday runs and one-weekend long run.

When thinking about your jog for work, home, family, friends, and personal playlist, I want you to think about a relaxed run, a jog where you steadily build endurance. It is an all-out workout in itself, but the jog also prepares you for more challenging races. For example, in the marathon, where you would have what we call race pace or marathon pace, where you increase speed the day of the marathon to beat your previously recorded time.

Work Jog

A jog is ideal when you have returned refreshed from your break and feel you can now elevate your jog by jumping right back in and tackling more of that "to-do" list or going back to a project or tasks you were working on right before you took your break. It's all about getting back into the groove; your mind instinctively wants to pick up from where it left off. To motivate you, I recommend Madonna's *Into the Groove* hit song. Start working at a leisurely pace and pick up momentum as you move through the remainder of your day.

Home Jog

Let's carry the "Into the Groove" theme into the home portion; we all have habits when we arrive home. It is our own personal groove, our personal flow of the way we are at home. You might immediately take your shoes off and put on comfy slippers, or your shoes stay on. You track the outside world in, and your shoes end up in some random place. Next, your socks are disbursed somewhere near the entryway on a shelf or the floor, then a sweater laid over a chair, and finally, your keys, purse, or wallet landing wherever they land. You can envision this happening to the music of the opening scene of the *Grease* movie. "Grease is the time, is the place, is the motion." Lyrics written by Barry Gibb and performed by Frankie Valli.

It seems to go perfectly for when you arrive home after a kickass day at the office, and while it's happening, it's all well and done. Let's listen to the lyrics again, "Grease is the time, is the place, is the motion."

Now don't get me wrong, *Grease* has one of the most iconic soundtracks of our time, and each song supports the storyline. But for now, I want us to capture the words that precede the above lyrics, "it's got groove, it's got meaning." When thinking about your groove, you've gotta be sure it's got meaning. By this, I want you to recognize that this is your home and that your groove has to have meaning; not only does it motivate, that it also supports efficiency in making your life easier. In the example that I gave above, about arriving home and dispensing articles of clothing, etcetera haphazardly, you're going to find yourself the next day tripping over your shoes, fighting with your dog because she has your sock in her mouth, and not being able to find your keys or wallet.

Each song is a great motivator to get things done, and I've been known to use a song or two in my spin class and while cleaning up my home. But for something to be as smooth as *Grease*, you've gotta plan and implement habits. Now let's try this again, "Grease is the time" you've just arrived home (place), you unlocked the door, your keys and wallet, go into a bin on the table next to your door, your shoes end up on a shoe rack, your socks come off, and your feet land in cozy slippers, and then your socks and clothes make it into the laundry hamper (motion). You've given meaning to the lyrics. This tiny jog home has made the rest of your day easier and the next day even easier.

So, whether it's Madonna's *In the Groove* or Frankie Valli's *Grease*, you'll slide directly into your home routine (groove).

Personal (Family & Friends) Jog

A jog in your personal life may be something of a transition to greater things; for example, many of us often make New Year's resolutions in pursuit of opportunities such as a new home, a new job, a new relationship, a healthier lifestyle, or many other workable obtainable goals. When I think about getting to my goals, I think about Whitney Houston's Step by Step lyrics:

"Step by step, bit by bit
Stone by Stone (yeah), brick by brick (oh yeah)
Step by step, day by day, mile by mile (ooh, ooh, ooh)"
Step by Step – Whitney Houston

As mentioned earlier, I've trained for marathons, and now is a good time to chat about the conditioning involved. In marathon training, we start with short runs and eventually progress to longer runs. With every step, trainees increase their confidence and endurance. Months of training are broken down into weekly segments consisting of mileage, speed intervals, and time; each is carefully planned to condition your body and allow the trainee to monitor and see progress. When I first started running and saw a marathon training plan for the first time, it scared me; all those weeks of training and the mileage I would accumulate seemed unobtainable. Heck, the first mile even frightened me, but following the plan worked, and I completed my first marathon and many more marathons. When wanting to reach a goal, such as changing careers, you will need to research to determine what will be required to obtain the goal. For this purpose, I will use the example of becoming a fitness instructor. I did my research by first asking fitness professionals I had already known to recommend places or entities that offered certification; next, I researched their recommendations for programs that

58

fit my existing schedule and timeline. This exploration process allowed me to jog first and then jump right in with the program's curriculum I selected. Noting that the curriculum, too, was designed like a marathon training plan, outlined to show progress towards certification, with foundational components of fitness taught first and then enhanced teachings on those components to further increase my knowledge to the level of a fitness professional. They were cumulating to one big test at the end that covered all that I had learned. When laid out like this, the path to becoming a fitness professional is straightforward. I must admit that not all paths will be as clear as you embark on obtaining your goals. Still, if you research and allow yourself some time, you can outline a path that works for you. The jog for meeting a goal would be something like this, set the goal, surround yourself with others who have already obtained the goal, find out how they did it, and determine the next steps, by deciding what is needed, education, connections, registrations, applications, whatever it may be, you must set a time to start and a time to end, filling in the steps between that start and end time.

Freestyle (Active Recovery)

Freestyle allows my riders an opportunity to digest what they've done and to align their own personal take to the rhythm of the music. I usually provide a song that I feel will encourage the rider to reflect on their day or encourage them to relate to the lyrics of the music. I've noted similarities with the timing of these types of songs with Cyclebar and Soul Cycle. Although they would refer to them with different terminology, I have labeled this type of song on my playlist as "Freestyle," informing participants that this is their opportunity to ride in or out of the saddle at any resistance they'd like, an active recovery of sorts.

Work Freestyle

Freestyle for your workday is an opportunity to let your mind and work go with their own natural flow. If that means checking on those emails, setting up meetings, checking out your work benefits, catching up on phone calls, or cruising through work tasks, then do it. The idea is that you shouldn't feel pressured during this time and that you allow your mind and body to inform you of what it wants to do. For me, I usually have "freestyle" worked into my calendar. Every week, I have time blocked out on my calendar where I list tasks that require follow-up. For example, if I send out an email with an open-ended response time and want to set a time to follow up on it, this would go into that designated time slot for that week. Freestyle is usually a time when I anticipate or have found that my meeting calendar for that day isn't full. At the same time, I don't feel inundated with multiple meetings throughout the day, and I don't have anxiety about preparing for those meetings. Since we're on this subject, and Freestyle begins with an "F," let's talk about another word that begins with an "F." Pause for thought....... Now get your mind outta the gutter; I'm talking about the word "Focus."

Ok, did I really include such a joke? I almost took it out of this paragraph but decided to leave it in for my own humor. Just another silly joke to keep you on your toes.

But getting back to focus, I occasionally add to my calendar a timeslot for focused workflow. This time is solely used when reviewing critical data, writing an email that requires further thought or working on creating or implementing a new process or idea. Focus is a great replacement for the Freestyle component. The follow-up list for the block of Freestyle time would look something like this.

— Call Dr. Smith regarding continuing medical education credits,

— Follow-up with vendor regarding go-live date.

— Send emails to staff members regarding upcoming projects.

— Set up my dog Cardi's grooming appointment.

— Call to refill mom's prescription.

Note that 4 & 5, although on work time, allows me to get some personal stuff done and feel that all is well in my personal world and can quickly remove my mindset from work for a bit, which is sometimes what we need.

Home Freestyle

Freestyle at home would be the task of cleaning out my closet. "I can have my Gucci on, I could wear my Louis Vuitton, but even with nothin' on, bet I made you look (I made you look)" *Made You Look*, Meghan Trainer (2022). When I hear this song, I am reminded of how many labels I do not own, by not owning many labels makes my life easier and gets me a step ahead in cleaning out my closet. I have many friends who prefer name brands, labels, and the most updated fashion pieces and are on an endless hunt for the next best thing or trending item. This task has always been easy for me, as I have always taken a conservative approach when purchasing clothing. That's not to say that I haven't overspent in the past; I'm definitely a sucker for t-shirts with fun quotes or graphics and basically anything unique on a t-shirt. I'm the type of guy who, if I find a t-shirt store that has great products, rarely do I share the name of the store when asked where did I get my shirt; I've gotta keep my uniqueness to myself, just kidding, here's where I get my t-shirts at, Strange Cargo and The Alley store, both in Chicago with a long history of providing fun shirts, and of course the chain stores, Spencer's, and Hot Topic.

Kohl's and Target have also been known to have some fun t-shirts. But by no means is this me advocating for you to go out and shop; after all, this is about minimizing what we own. But wouldn't the world be a much better place if everyone wore fun t-shirts all the time?

Imagine your boss in a "Kiss" shirt, rocking to music in the office. I've always been a t-shirt and jeans type of guy, but some years ago, in an effort to downsize my belongings, I had to learn the hard lesson of getting rid of stuff, and by no means was this easy. When I decided to downsize, it was way before Marie Kondo's *The Life-Changing Magic of Tidying Up: The Japanese Art of Decluttering and Organizing*, whereas a lot of my influence came from *Simplifying your Life*, by Elizabeth St. James, which I mentioned early in this book, but would like to quote with "a giant step on the road to simplicity is to eliminate the odds and end that clutter up your home, your car, your office, and your life." Taking this to heart, I could identify those odds and ends and simplify all three major components in this book of work, home, family, and friends, yes, friends, because let's face it, some friends do not spark joy. Although I was exposed to Marie Kondo's "Does this spark joy" method later in life, it has helped me tremendously eliminate clutter in my work, home, and life. But even with my background and understanding of decluttering, I did find that I was still holding on to more than I wanted to. So staying current with new trends or processes that I can add to my already existing decluttering habits has helped me in staying on top of my minimalist journey.

Now back to my clothes, being annoyed with the frustration of having to figure out what to wear, and the possibility of someone seeing me in the same cool *Ed Hardy* t-shirt twice in the same week, I began to opt for just wearing a white or black t-shirt as I did in the 80s and 90s, minus the black motorcycle jacket. Hmm, I might need to start wearing a motorcycle jacket again; note to self, find one at a vintage store. By limiting myself to black or white t-shirts, I immediately eliminated the frustration of what to wear and made it easier to get dressed and out the door; I'm a stickler for being on time. Don't get me wrong; I didn't jump off the deep end and get rid of all my cool t-shirts; I still wear them to this day, with holes and stains. I wear them with the intention for the person, place, or event I'd be attending.

Reevaluating your clothes is a great habit to have. Recently, at a monthly game night with my buddies, a friend mentioned that since it was the end of summer, I'd need to get rid of the shirts that I wore to various festivals all summer, stating that people would notice if I wore the same t-shirt again the next summer. Did I follow his advice? No, but I did donate my "Adios Felicia" shirt because it had run its course and would grace the chest of someone else who might find it entertaining. I put this task of cleaning out the closet in the freestyle component of your playlist because this will become a consistent natural habit in your life and something that, once done, you'll be able to easily do every time.

Next, I'd like to bring to mind two highly publicized people in our culture, Steve Jobs and Mark Zuckerberg. If you Google images of them, you'll notice that in most photos, their choice of clothing is the same; for Jobs, it's a black turtleneck and jeans; for Zuckerberg, it's a white t-shirt and jeans. Additionally, as Megan Trainer's lyrics at the beginning of this portion stated, they're gonna look anyway.

Bonus: When I started working in fitness, I found that I always chose to wear black ankle socks or black gym socks; both went well with my choice of footwear. I also noticed that these black socks also went with the shoes and slacks I wore to the office. To make my life easier, I got rid of all my white socks and dress socks and only kept a couple with cute designs.

.

Personal (Family & Friends) Freestyle

In Taylor Swift's song *Blank Space*, she mentions that she has "a blank space and I'll write your name". I know that earlier I mentioned keeping white space on your calendar, but you should allow yourself the freedom to add a name to the list as you wish. There's a certain type of comfort in having the flexibility to allow for more joy with your family and friends. Another song that comes to mind is Cody Johnson's *Till You Can't*.

"You can tell your old man, you'll do some large-mouth fishing another time, you just got too much on your plate, to bait and catch a line…Til you can't…You can keep putting off forever with that girl whose heart you hold, swearing that you'll ask someday further down the road. You can always put a diamond on her hand, Til you can't."

There's not more that I can say here, but that to trust your intuition and go with the flow. Make time for those family and friends that you have prioritized.

Intervals

We've all heard the term multitasking, and we've either added it to our resume or seen it on resumes. But I believe that actual multitasking doesn't exist where total concentration on one project or situation is required; I say this because some projects require 100 percent focus, and some situations require 100 percent participation. In reality, we shift our attention from one task to another. Very similar to an interval in spin may be that you're in the saddle at 80-90 rpm and then out of the saddle at 65-75 rpm. Essentially two different tasks which you can't do at the same time.

Work Intervals

Depending on the type of work you do, intervals are predetermined by the projects or cyclic events that encompass your day. Intervals at work require planning and time; this is where your calendar comes in handy.

You can set up intervals throughout your day that require you to jump back and forth from one project to the next. For example, suppose I am working with large sets of data. In that case, I often will block out time on my calendar that says "focus" using the same methodology that I used in the Freestyle component above, for example, three hours, with a timer set on my desk for every 45 minutes and 15-minute intervals, allowing me to break up the monotony by taking a 15-minute break or doing a task that requires less concentration, preferably not email since this might require that I reply to a message, and get lost in email, taking more than the allotted 15 minutes.

An example of this is the Jeff Galloway *Run Walk Method*, where you run for 3 minutes and walk for one minute.

Home Intervals

When it comes to home intervals (organization), I want you to think about opportunities to create a multipurpose space. As in the bike set-up chapter, I mention that for some folks, their homes have also become their place of work. In many cases, newly remote work-from-home employees have learned to multipurpose their homes. For example, a spare bedroom now serves as a multipurpose extra bedroom/home office.

Those who don't have that luxury have carved out work spaces out of existing spaces. For example, while chatting with friends, the array of workspaces is now on dining room tables, the corner part of kitchen islands, and closets fashioned to be workspaces that can easily be closed off. Suppose you have a closet that can easily be converted. In that case, this is definitely a bonus, as this will allow you to hide your workspace without giving up another space in a different room. For current design inspiration with the work-from-home era we live in, I recommend checking out Apartment Therapy at www.apartmenttherapy.com; it is a great resource.

While getting organized, many folks immediately believe that to do so, you have to buy items that promise to solve all your organization and storage challenges. Many people run out and buy totes, bins, baskets, bookcases, shelves, food containers, etc. Don't get me wrong; I own some of the above organizational items, but I want you to think about alternatives to immediately buying such items.

Simplifying your home shouldn't require acquiring more material things to house your existing things; it should be about eliminating and only keeping what is necessary. The only acquisition you should make is to acquire knowledge and only buy if the item truly serves a purpose and ultimately eliminates clutter, not just a pretty box to mask what you are trying or should get rid of.

When I purchase something, I think about its use in a multipurpose format—for example, buying a bookcase with a handy desk built-in or an old antique secretary's desk. Both provide storage and a place to work and can be aesthetically pleasing. Baskets, for example, can provide quick access to something you often use, such as bathroom necessities like towels, toilet paper, and other things you would want access to. Since floor space is often in short supply in my multipurpose office/workout rooms, I have outfitted my multipurpose room with wall shelves. Wall shelves have allowed me to display books (the ones I have decided to keep, knick-knacks that are important to me, some photos, and anything else I might need).

Additionally, I have also opted for IKEA'S narrow *Billy Bookcases*, which have a height of 84 inches, 11 inches in depth, and approximately 16 inches in width, and six shelves to display whatever it is that I need. The Billy bookcases usually contain my fitness, minimalist, Buddhism, and self-help books. I list the measurements because when designing your space, it is important to know how much space you're working with. You'd be surprised how much you can fit into small spaces and the options afforded to you when you understand how much space you have. Wall shelves and narrow Billy bookcases have given me my floorspace back.

Personal (Family & Friends) Intervals

Multitasking may work better here as you can easily create opportunities to spend time with family and friends while achieving other tasks. For example, when cooking, I enjoy having a family member assist; this time together allows us to chat and catch up. When my kids were younger, they'd sit at the kitchen table while I prepared dinner, and now and then, I would work with them on a math problem on the dry-erase board that hung next to my kitchen stove.

Multi-purposing the kitchen in this way helped us to bond, get homework done, and allowed them to sometimes help in meal prep if they did their homework. The above scenarios are nothing new; the dry-erase board may be, but families and friends have gathered in the kitchen for ages. That's why gathering in the kitchen at a family or friend event seems much more enjoyable; you can cook your favorite dish and still talk to your bestie who needs your time. You'll also notice that at most parties, most folks gravitate toward the kitchen.

Let's dive deeper into intervals with family and friends. We have all had that hurried schedule that requires us to be in two places simultaneously and have commitments overlap. Sometimes this is unavoidable, but you can definitely get a hold on your time by prioritizing your commitments to be fully present and eliminate those commitments that no longer serve you. You can divide your time by scheduling time to hang with all your children at once or by creating unique opportunities for each child for one-on-one time.

Additionally, you can look at your existing schedule and enhance existing commitments by using those drives to soccer practice to chat about your kids' school day; however, don't be surprised if they tune you out. Heck, they need their time too, and with their busy schedules of school, sports, extracurricular activities, friends, and family, they are looking for a way to disconnect and find balance too. So set the example and get your life in order by demonstrating healthy relationships, boundaries, and hobbies that nurture your mind and soul. One interval that I like to do when it comes to my friends is that I usually have a close friend that I hang out with for a Sunday Funday. Sometimes it's great just the two of us having a blast running into friends at our local restaurants and bars, chatting up the bartenders. Still, now and then, we invite a ton of other close friends along and find a nice cozy spot at the bar where we can all gather. Catch-up—finding time to all laugh and take turns pitching to buy a run of drinks or helping to carry a round of drinks from the bar, allowing you a bit of time to catch up with the friend buying the drinks or if you're the one buying drinks. Naturally, you'll find that folks don't always tend to sit in the same chair, changing their position throughout the day, or at the next bar, make an effort to stand next to someone you couldn't chat with at the previous bar. Something like this would be considered an interval and a great way of multitasking the desire to spend time with friends. An opportunity like this will allow you to feel some contentment in having spent time with those important to you.

If all else fails, invite your friends over and "Let's have a kiki... a kiki is a partee for calming all your nerves," *Let's Have a Kiki* -Sister Scissors. A party is always a great way to get everyone together.

Bonus: "One ring to rule them all" In J.R.R. Tolkien's *The Lord of the Rings* and *The Hobbit*, the ring had the power to rule them all, essentially having the power of many. For all intended purposes, when editing your space, start to think about the tools you use. Which tools will serve many purposes and have the most impact? For example, when I think about pocket knives, some are very simple with a knife, corkscrew, nail file, and keychain, while others carry many more features. In addition to the above, some pocket knives boast screwdrivers, Allen wrenches, and multipronged tools; hell, I've even seen some with flashlights. When I started to look at my space, I noticed that in my new office space, I did many other things; it was a place to meditate in front of my tranquil Buddha sculpture and thriving plants, a place where I could practice on my 88-piano keyboard, a place to work, and a place to write. For all these purposes, I had a different chair for each, a small stool for meditation, an antique piano stool, and a gaming chair as an office chair.

With limited space, I constantly moved each seat around, banging the gaming chair against other pieces of furniture and tucking out-of-use seats between spaces and crevices. Having so many chairs was chaotic and unsightly; eventually, the gaming chair didn't provide enough back support for sitting upright at a desk. As my back began to suffer, I felt it was time to buy a new chair. During the shopping process, I considered this an opportunity to address the functional needs the chair would need to meet. I eventually settled on a backless laboratory-grade stool with quick height adjustments that rolled. The versatility and design of the stool allowed it to become the only chair in the space. I used it to meditate, sit at the desk, and then at the piano keyboard for practice. This one chair allowed me to free up space and donate the extra seating to a local charity. Using the wall shelves I mentioned earlier allowed me to create additional lighting by placing battery-operated puck lights under the shelve that was immediately above my work monitor and laptop, creating more ambient light in my workspace. I essentially found myself setting the physical stage for a more effective workspace. You see, eventually, with the monitor on the wall and the laptop and mouse being the only electronic items on my desk, I could quickly remove them and put my personal laptop, sewing machine, or art projects on the desk, making my desk a multiuse tool. What can you scale back on, and what might you be able to identify as a multipurpose tool in your home? As mentioned earlier, I installed the elevated wall shelves, which currently hold a small flatscreen television, plants, books, limited knickknacks, art, and other mementos.

Working smarter, not harder, still stands true no matter the climate. As mentioned in the Dua Lipa portion, where we organized our phone apps, this chapter follows the same guidelines of finding the right tools and bringing them to the forefront to make a big difference. This concept in this interval component can be applied to all facets of your life, in the kitchen, the bathroom, the bedroom, and the living room.

Double Bonus: A calendar can be a great tool. Recently, I purchased a calendar that has all of the things that I needed within a calendar.

First, it is visually appealing, with one regular wall-size calendar and four sub-calendars of the same month.

The full-size calendar currently has my daily word count for this book. The additional four smaller two-by-three-inch calendars have various associated habits, allowing me to "X" out the day if I completed the habit. The current four are Mediation, Fitness Practice, Outdoor Run, and Piano. The calendar serves as a multifunction tool and also serves as a visual representation of my real-life intervals. Sometimes old school paper and pen can meet the needs in our overly complicated technological world.

Cooldown

Work Cooldown

As mentioned earlier in this book, a spin class, like your workday, has a beginning and an end. Make sure that the start and end of your workday are identifiable; as mentioned earlier, this can be challenging for folks working from home. Having a routine that disconnects you from your working hours is essential. Besides shutting down my computer and leaving my workspace, I take a moment to recognize what I've accomplished for the day and take a deep breath while relieving the tension in my shoulders, gently pressing on my eyes to ease the tension from having looked at a computer screen most of the day, and then fully exhaling to close the chapter of the work day and begin my evening with the intent of finding balance for the remainder of the day. Your time away from work is one big break, and you should use it to replenish your state of mind and physical health.

Home Cooldown

As mentioned above, you should use your break from work wisely, many times while we are home, we tend to fall into set routines of watching a bit of television, listening to the radio, or getting lost in a book; all of these are great in moderation if it makes you happy, I say do it. However, when you're ready to wind down for the evening, it's good to have a habit such as having a timer set that will alert you to turn the television off, not look at your phone, brush and floss your teeth, and ease into your night by meditating or reading before bed, anything that will help you further disconnect and prepare you for a restful night's sleep. Sometimes I have anxiety when it's time for bed, and I can't sleep; I literally find myself "tossin' and turnin' all night," just like in Bobby Lewis' song *Tossin' and Turnin'*. Usually, this anxiety kicks in when I have to record a fitness demonstration for a new certification, work on a big project for work, or deal with challenging family matters. I have recently started saying to myself, "I give myself permission to sleep," and I have found that this has helped me tremendously.

Personal (Family & Friends) Cooldown

End on a good note. As much as possible, end every interaction with family and friends on a good note, even when there is strife. Be sure to say "I Love You," and if you were wrong about something, recognize when you are wrong, and apologize—follow up on any outstanding issues, concerns, etcetera.

Finish Strong (Not a Component but a State of Mind) – this applies to your whole ride, whatever you do, learn as much as you can, leave stronger and more knowledgeable than when you started and always make a lasting impression and give thanks for the experience you've gained.

Please see the example templates for creating your playlist (routine) on the next page. Please note that an actual spin class can take anywhere from 10-15 songs, depending on the length of the spin class.

Example Templates			
Work - Daily	Home - Over a Week or Month	Personal - Over a Week, Month, or Year	Goals - Set a Goal Completion Length
Warm-up	Warm-up	Warm-up	Warm-up
Climb	Jog	Jog	Jog
Jog	Sprint	Sprint	Break
Break	Break	Break	Freestyle
Speed	Interval	Interval	Interval
Jog	Jog	Freestyle	Jog
Break	Break	Jog	Speed
Climb	Jog	Break	Freestyle
Freestyle	Speed	Jog	Climb
Cooldown	Cooldown	Cooldown	Cooldown

Chapter Eight - What's Next? GROW

"Celebrate good times, come on! (Let's Celebrate.
There's a party goin' on right here
A celebration to last throughout the years
So bring your good times, and your laughter too
We gonna celebrate your party with you"
Celebration – Kool & The Gang

G- Group Fitness

There's a whole world of group fitness out there to explore. Don't stop at spin, although you can if you'd like to, but participating in multiple formats will help you grow. The same goes for your home and personal life; there are so many ways to live that you should continue to evolve. For example, in fitness, you should start engaging with your colleagues, family, and friends, find out what fitness activities they participate in, and ask if you can join. You might find that you have common goals and strengthen existing bonds. Recently, a friend invited me to go climbing at a climbing gym here in Chicago, which I usually avoid due to my fear of heights.

But I decided to challenge myself, and guess what? I've conquered my fear of heights and seen my strength and endurance challenged differently. Use this concept of engaging with family, friends, colleagues, and new associates to grow in other facets of your life.

R – Reassess

Now's a great time to reassess where you were and where you're at; take what you've learned and apply and continue to seek out new knowledge.

O – Organize

As you take on new goals and challenges, continue to organize your day and life. Most will fall into place, but a bit of strategy goes a long way.

W – Wins = Celebration

Now's a great time to hit play on Kool and the Gang's "Celebration." Celebrate every win when you can. Give yourself that proverbial pat on the back. We often accomplish goals and mark them off our list but we need to take the time to celebrate.

Mini-Chapter (It)

This chapter is so mini that "it" doesn't get a number. When creating your playlists for work, home, and life, I want you to think about the five "ITs." The "IT's" that have helped me throughout my fitness career and life.

The first is edIT; continue to edIT your playlist until it becomes as efficient as possible, allowing for flexibility. Second, fake IT till you make IT (third), and continue to move forward. Fourth is to master IT, master the skills necessary to accomplish your goals, and lastly, if all else fails, call your IT (information technology) department.

You may have noticed that "it" has parentheses in the title of the book; it really is about "working (it) out" in all facets of your life, a mini-chapter to support my overall concept.

Chapter Nine - Gratitude (A Moment of Reflection)

Find songs that move you and place them within your playlists to allow moments for reflection. This component doesn't exist in a spin class; however, songs that allow us to express our gratitude exist. In my spin classes, I have played songs that speak to me and allow me to express gratitude to my riders.

Gratitude for Work

Take this time to reflect on your day to find peace with what is, and by that, I mean finding happiness in the fact that you are employed, that you are being paid for your expertise, that having a job allows you to provide for yourself and if relevant for your family. In some cases, your job may not be your passion, but having gratitude for it will make having it a joy. What you haven't finished today, will be there tomorrow and you should only look at what you have accomplished in that given day. Find gratitude in all of your accomplishments, because you have gotten here through your hard work and determination.

Gratitude for Home

Find gratitude in your home, the fact that it shelters you, keeps "you and yours," those you love safe, provides a gathering place for family and friends, is a testament to all your hard work, a place that you have created, that is greater than the stuff we give away, collect, and hold onto. As an added bonus, I'd like to mention that recently I gave gratitude for having a parking space at home in a dense area in Chicago, where finding parking is a challenge, then this led to me having gratitude for having the comfort of a car.

Gratitude for Family & Friends

Gratitude for your family and friends, for the imperfectness of relationships, the subtle way relationships grow, the way that we are strengthened even by the most challenging of relationships. The understanding that although we may have to limit time with toxic individuals that they have contributed to some form of growth for us. That we can learn from each other, and that love comes in many forms. For all of this I have gratitude. I have gratitude for every year extra that I have, where I live beyond the years my dad and brother had on this earth. I am also grateful for the time that I had with them, I miss them, and still honor lessons that they and their lives have taught me.

Personal Moment for Gratitude & Closing Statement

Everyday that I wake up I have extreme gratitude for a new day. Every time I am able to teach a fitness class, I am grateful for the opportunity to create change. Every time I am inspired by a new song, I am grateful for new art being creative. Every time I make a new connection with someone, I am grateful for new beginnings. I am grateful for my mind, body, and soul. I am grateful to all of you who have taken the time to read this book.

Every year my runners the *Chicago Brunching Bandits* and I work on our marathon training plan schedule; we consider which marathons participants will run in and then plan accordingly. Set the stage for your goals by identifying how you will get there.

It's ok to live for a bit in the fantasy of an idea, but now's the time to make it happen, get out there, and do it. Shift and change perspective; being able to pivot is important.

Another idea I'd like to share is that this book was about you and protecting your personal space, creating opportunities, efficiencies, and templates for improved performance.

But I also want to address something else that is just as important in healthy relationships at work, at home, and in life. It's really quite simple, "if you make a mistake, take responsibility for it, and mend those relationships you have, but most importantly, mend the relationship you have with yourself."

Mending the relationship with myself would be recognizing that for this book, many ideas would pop-up and I would want to add more to an already existing manuscript in an effort for perfection and to cover as much material as possible. I had to let go, and allow myself to move forward, and not let the pursuit of perfection get in the way of publishing.

Bonus Gratitude:

To my brother Alex, thank you for being a part of my life for my first 23 years, and although we lost you in a tragedy, I have found gratitude for having the opportunity to become a dad and raise two of your children and now co-parent with their mom.

To my dad, the night before you transitioned to your eternal rest, when one of my best friends and I stayed the night to watch over you and when you were coughing, and I was getting up to help you, my friend said, "let me help, let me take care of him." This act of kindness on her part led you to tell me that you were so tough on me because you were afraid of my big heart and that you were trying to protect me from getting hurt, and that the act of kindness from my friend demonstrated my ability to surround myself with love. Hearing that from you gave me the peace I had been searching for. Additionally, thank you for showing me the foundation of what a good father is during the limited 28 years we've had together.

The above two bonus gratitude statements almost didn't make it into the book, but I believe that they both demonstrate that although we can suffer great loss, that we can still find gratitude.

Music Recommendations

Here are 70 songs; I have extensive music playlists. I couldn't narrow it done any further because I wanted to give you a snippet of music and associated possible combinations to components of a ride. Please note that depending on which beat per minute (BPM) you pick up on, each song can serve multiple components of a ride. Here's a list from Spotify.

Warm-up		
Song	**Artist**	**Year**
Beautiful Day	U2	2000
Dirrty (feat. Redman)	Christina Aguilera	2002
When I Grow Up	The Pussycat Dolls	2008
I Gotta Feeling	Black Eyed Peas	2009
All the Lovers	Kylie Minogue	2010
Firework	Katy Perry	2010
Timebomb	Kylie Minogue	2012
Dance Again	Jennifer Lopez	2012
Delicate	Taylor Swift	2017
We Got Love - Glammstar Remix	Jessica Mauboy	2018

Hill - Climb

Song	Artist	Year
Don't Cha	The Pussycat Dolls	2005
Push	Madonna	2005
Brokenhearted	Karmin	2012
Confident	Demi Lovato	2015
What The Funk	Kat Graham	2017
I Don't Know Why	Imagine Dragons	2017
Caramelo Duro (feat. Kali Uchis)	Miguel	2017
Pynk (feat. Grimes)	Janelle Monáe	2018
Girls (feat. Cardi B, Bebe Rexha & Charli XCX)	Rita Ora	2018
Deep Water	American Authors	2018
Boys	Lizzo	2019

Dash - Race - Speed - Sprint

Song	Artist	Year
Dive In The Pool (feat. Pepper Mashay) - Radio Edit	Barry Harris	2001
Diva - Karmatronic Club Remix	Beyoncé	2009
I Look to You - Johnny Vicious Warehouse Radio Mix	Whitney Houston	2009
Not Myself Tonight	Christina Aguilera	2010
Give Me Everything (feat. Ne-Yo, Afrojack & Nayer)	Pitbull	2011
Crank It Up (feat. Akon)	David Guetta	2011
I Love It (feat. Charli XCX)	Icona Pop	2012
Work Bitch	Britney Spears	2013
Silence - Tiësto's Big Room Remix	Marshmello	2017
Flamenco (feat. Rage)	Timmy Trumpet	2018

Jog		
Song	**Artist**	**Year**
I'm an Albatraoz	AronChupa	2014
Last Dance - Single Version	Donna Summer	1978
Move Ya Body	Nina Sky	2004
SexyBack (feat. Missy Elliott & Timbaland) - DJ Wayne Williams Ol' Skool Remix	Justin Timberlake	2006
Indian Summer	Jai Wolf	2015
Hell Nos And Headphones	Hailee Steinfeld	2016
Into You	Ariana Grande	2016
Treat You Better	Shawn Mendes	2016
Chained To The Rhythm	Katy Perry	2017
Mi Gente	J Balvin	2017
I Like It	Cardi B	2018

Freestyle		
Song	**Artist**	**Year**
The Reason	Hoobastank	2004
Chasing Cars	Snow Patrol	2006
No One	Alicia Keys	2007
Yo No Sé Mañana	Luis Enrique	2009
Heroes (we could be)	Alesso	2014
Paris	The Chainsmokers	2017
Sunny Days	Armin van Buuren	2017
All I Am	Jess Glynne	2018
What They'll Say About Us	FINNEAS	2020
Above the Clouds	Amber	1999

Intervals		
Song	**Artist**	**Year**
Pump Up the Jam	Technotronic	1998
Lose Control (feat. Ciara & Fat Man Scoop)	Missy Elliott	2005
Teeth	Lady Gaga	2009
Run the World (Girls)	Beyoncé	2011
Work - Freemasons Radio Edit	Kelly Rowland	2011
Feva (Ranny's Radio Edit) [feat. Deepa Soul]	Ranny	2013
Booty	Jennifer Lopez	2014
Clap Snap	Icona Pop	2015
TERRITORY	The Blaze	2017
Kumbaza	Chuckie	2017

Cooldown		
Song	**Artist**	**Year**
Beethoven's 5 Secrets	The Piano Guys	2012
The Cello Song	The Piano Guys	2012
Faded	Alan Walker	2015
Migrants	Federico Albanese	2016
Escape! (from "The Hours")	Philip Glass	2017
Perfect	Ed Sheeran	2017
Rewrite the Stars	Benj Pasek	2018
A Million Dreams	Benj Pasek	2018
Ceremony of Innocence - EastWest Session	Moby	2018
Prisma (Acoustic)	Dardust	2019

References

Clear, James. *Atomic Habits. Avery,* 2017.

Bittman, Mark. "A No-Frills Kitchen Still Cooks." *The New York Times,* 9 May 2007, www.nytimes.com/2007/05/09/dining/09mini.html. Accessed 8 Feb. 2023.

Blake Johnson, Nicole. "WHY YOUR CALENDAR NEEDS MORE WHITE SPACE." *Govloop,* 27 Feb. 2020, www.govloop.com/why-your-calendar-needs-more-white-space/. Accessed 8 Feb. 2023.

Bourdain, Anthony. *Kitchen Confidential Updated Edition: Adventures in the Culinary Underbelly (P.S.). Ecco,* 2007.

Brown, Brene, host. Dare to Lead, Spotify, 19 Oct. 2020.

Combiths, Shifrah. "The 20-Minute Dailly Routine That'Ll Give You Your Weekends Back." *Apartment Therapy,* 11 Jul. 2017, www.apartmenttherapy.com/this-20-minute-daily-clean-routine-will-give-you-your-weekends-back-247491. Accessed 8 Feb. 2023.

de Becker, Gavin. *The Gift of Fear: And Other Survival Signals That Protect Us from Violence. Dell,* 1998.

Duckworth, Angela. *Grit: The Power of Passion and Perseverance.* 1st ed., *Scribner,* 2016.

Friedman, Ron. "How to Spend the First 10 Minutes of Your Day." *Harvard Business Review,* 19 Jun. 2014, hbr.org/2014/06/how-to-spend-the-first-10-minutes-of-your-day. Accessed 8 Feb. 2023.

Harris, Susan, Junger Witt, Paul, and Thomas, Tony, creators. *The Golden Girls.* Witt/Thomas/Harris Productions and Touchstone Television, 1985.

Johnson, Whitney, host. Disrupt Yourself, Spotify, 21 Sep. 2016.

Kassel, Gabrielle. "What 'Chosen Family' Means — And How to Build Your Own." *Healthline*, 9 Jun. 2021, www.healthline.com/health/relationships/chosen-family. Accessed 8 Feb. 2023.

Knight, Sarah. *The Life-Changing Magic of Not Giving a F*Ck*. *Voracious*, 2015.

Kondo, Marie. *The Life-Changing Magic of Tidying Up: The Japanese Art of Decluttering and Organizing*. 1st ed., *Ten Speed Press*, 2014.

"Merriam-Webster." *Merriam-Webster Est. 1828*, 8 Feb. 2023, www.merriam-webster.com. Accessed 8 Feb. 2023.

Obama, Michelle. *Becoming*. 1st ed., *Crown*, 2018.

Piper, Watty. *The Little Engine That Could*. *Golden Books*, 1980.

Sex and the City. Directed by Michael Patrick King, New Line Cinema, 2008.

Sinek, Simon, host. "Service with Maria Shriver." A Bit of Optimism, Spotify, 22 Jun. 2020.

St James, Elaine. *Simplify Your Life: 100 Ways to Slow Down and Enjoy the Things That Really Matter*. 1st ed., *Hachette Books*, 2017.

The Devil Wears Prada. Directed by David Frankel, 20th Century Fox, 2006.

Tolkien, J.R.R. *J.R.R. Tolkien 4-Book Boxed Set: The Hobbit and The Lord of the Rings*. *Del Rey*, 2010.

Tracey, Brian. *Eat That Frog!: 21 Great Ways to Stop Procrastinating and Get More Done in Less*. 3rd ed., *Berrett-Koehler Publishers*, 2017.

Musical References

— Beyonce.
"Irreplacable." *Spotify*. https://open.spotify.com/search/to%20the%20left.

— Black Eyed Peas. "I Gotta Feeling." *Spotify*. https://open.spotify.com/search/I%20Gotta%20Feeling.

— Depeche Mode. "Walking in My Shoes - 2006 Remaster." *Spotify*. https://open.spotify.com/search/Walking%20in%20My%20Shoes%20-%202006%20Remaster

— Gaynor, Gloria. "I Will Survive - Original 7" Version." *Spotify*. https://open.spotify.com/search/I%20Will%20Survive%20-%20Original%207%22%20Version.

— Houston, Whitney. "I Look to You - Johnny Vicious Warehouse Radio Mix." *Spotify*. https://open.spotify.com/search/I%20Look%20to%20You%20-%20Johnny%20Vicious%20Warehouse%20Radio%20Mix

— James, Etta. "Something's Got A Hold On Me - Live." *Spotify*. https://open.spotify.com/search/etta%20james%20somethings%20gott

— Johnson, Cody. "Til You Can't." *Spotify*. https://open.spotify.com/search/'Til%20You%20Can't.

— Kool & The Gang. "Celebration - Single Version." *Spotify*. https://open.spotify.com/search/Celebration%20-%20Single%20Version

— Lipa, Dua. "New Rules." *Spotify*. https://open.spotify.com/search/New%20Rules.

— Madonna. "Into the Groove." *Spotify*. https://open.spotify.com/search/Into%20the%20Groove

— Run–D.M.C.. "It's Like That." *Spotify*. https://open.spotify.com/search/It's%20Like%20That.

— Scissor Sisters. "Let's Have A Kiki." *Spotify*. https://open.spotify.com/search/Let's%20Have%20A%20Kiki

— Simone, Nina. "Why? (The King Of Love Is Dead) - Unedited version from original live concert." *Spotify*. https://open.spotify.com/artist/7G1GBhoKtEPnP86X2PvEYO.

— Spears, Britney. "Toxic." *Spotify*. https://open.spotify.com/search/Toxic

— Spice Girls. "Spice Up Your Life." *Spotify*. https://open.spotify.com/search/spice%20up%20your%20life

— Swift, Taylor. "Blank Space." *Spotify*. https://open.spotify.com/search/Blank%20Space.

— The Bangles. "Manic Monday." *Spotify*. https://open.spotify.com/search/Manic%20Monday

— The Chainsmokers (Ballerini, Kelsee). "This Feeling." *Spotify*. https://open.spotify.com/search/This%20Feeling.

— Timmy Trumphet. "Oracle." *Spotify*. https://open.spotify.com/search/Oracle

— Trainor, Meghan. "Made You Look." *Spotify*. https://open.spotify.com/search/Made%20You%20Look.

— Turner, Tina. "Proud Mary." *Spotify*. https://open.spotify.com/search/Proud%20Mary

— Twain, Shania. "Up!." *Spotify*. https://open.spotify.com/search/Up!%20shania.

— Vallie, Frankie. "Grease - From "Grease"." *Spotify*. https://open.spotify.com/search/Grease%20-%20From%20%E2%80%9CGrease%E2%80%9D

— Whitney Houston. "Step by Step." *Spotify*. https://open.spotify.com/search/Step%20by%20Step.

Resources for Music

— Spotify
— Apple Music
— Prime Music
— IHeart Radio
— YouTube
— Old school vinyl (records), cassettes, 8-tracks, compact discs, mp3s, and Old School Radio Stations (this is my dad humor).

Honorable Mentioned

Les Mills, Soul Cycle, Cyclebar, Peloton, Chicago Athletic Clubs, Target, Kohl's, Strange Cargo Chicago, Target, Madd Dogg Spinning, American Council on Exercise, Road Runners Club of America, Jeff Galloway Run Walk Program, Michael's, Amazon, Fuel Rewards, Blick , Dolly, Yelp, Facebook, Instagram, NikeRun, Garmin, Gmail, AOL Google, Chicago Marathon, Redfin, Zillow, Ed Hardy, Steve Jobs, Mark Zuckerberg, Ikea

Made in the USA
Monee, IL
13 February 2023

27688303R00056